What It's Like To Be Alive

SELECTED POEMS

What It's Like To Be Alive

SELECTED POEMS

Deryn Rees-Jones

SEREN

Seren is the book imprint of
Poetry Wales Press Ltd.
57 Nolton Street, Bridgend, Wales, CF31 3AE
www.serenbooks.com
facebook.com/SerenBooks
twitter@SerenBooks

The right of Deryn Rees-Jones to be identified as
the author of this work has been asserted in accordance
with the Copyright, Designs and Patents Act, 1988.

ISBN: 978-1-78172-338-8
E-book: 978-1-78172-345-6
Kindle: 978-1-78172-346-3

A CIP record for this title is available from the British Library.

The publisher acknowledges the financial assistance of the Welsh Books Council.

Cover Artwork: 'Flying Children' by Paula Rego, 1992, © Paula Rego, Courtesy
Marlborough Fine Art.

Printed by Latimer Trend & Company Ltd, Plymouth.

Author Website: www.derynrees-jones.co.uk

Contents

from *Quiver*

I

II

III

from *Burying the Wren*

from *The Memory Tray* (1994)

The Great Mutando

Pulls rabbits out of hats,
ties up the day with handkerchiefs in silk.

So many colours make me cry.
Ladies and Gentlemen, for my next trick!

He spins the earth,
blues, greens, a plate

on a stick.
Punch. Judy.

Five silver glistening rings
that link

then come apart.
Six doves.

Five fly, one suffocates.
A little drop of shit

runs down his sleeve.
He makes a dachshund from

three pink balloons.
Mutando!

I want a name like that.
and a world.

Wands. Fairy godmothers.
No crocodiles.

A place where I can get
the handkerchiefs to knot.

Iconographies

*It would be truly marvellous if I were thus able to create illness
at the pleasure of my whim and caprice. But as for the truth,
I am absolutely only the photographer; I register what I see.*
                                                    –J.M. Charcot

Empty as a seashell, I give myself to you entirely,
lost in the curve of my own fantastic echo. I am
as far away from myself as ever I thought I could
possibly be and live, stretched out on a pale horizon
where a gap grows like a thin blue line
between the blue sky and the too blue sea....

I am X, the unknown quantity. I am Augustine.
I am Louise. At night I dream of rape and fire. I will
tell you my age quietly. Fifteen. *Take me
I'm yours.* This is my *supplication amoureuse*:
my hair's tossed back and my hands are raised.
I am beautiful, irresistible as a prayer. Later

I will perform, suck charcoal
like a chocolate bar. On all fours
I will shove up my skirts for you,
bark like a dog; your soft kid glove
becomes a snake in the time it takes
for you to simply say the words and

throw it to the floor. I'm not afraid
I scream. I carry your top hat, kissing
the line of its wet black silks
as if it were a child (my child, your child,
perhaps it is our child that I hold
between us, a bond of the mind.) You touch me often,

maître, and it hurts. *La Salpêtrière*. My eyes roll
and my body shudders. I am a pigeon or an eagle
or a dove. For one glorious moment I
am learning to fly. You love me, you love me not.
I am your Tuesday star. Sarah Bernhardt
's my heroine. I've never seen her but I hear her face

is perfect and her voice is pure. And now
I am a walking miracle. With a flash
you take my photograph. By now I
only see the world in black and white.
I smile. *Life is an art*. Like everything else, I do it.

The Memory Tray

The language game 'I am afraid' already contains the object.
—Wittgenstein

There was a milk tooth, with the string that pulled it.
There was a letter in your father's hand.
Welcome to the real world.
There was a chocolate heart wrapped in red tin foil.
There was, *embarrassment,*
a contraceptive, a sanitary towel.
There was a can of laughter.
Can you remember?

Remember I remember I remember.
There was a photograph of somebody I never knew
but knew the name of. There was a tiny paper box,
so beautiful. There was an object
that I can't quite place. Here, instead,
is my dream. I remember it in order: (1) *a big man*
(2) *with his big hands* (3) *in a maze who*
sees (4) *a flock of birds, then*
stoops (5) *to tie his shoes, his fingers*
(6's and 7's) *fingering the laces sadly*
like the drooping heads of flowers....

William and Georgie, 1917

*...the sheer volume of scripts Mrs Yeats preserved made an
impressive sight...*
                    –A. Norman Jeffares: *W.B. Yeats: A New Biography*

She is wearing a coat of rainbow camel-hair
and a rose-quartz crystal round her neck.
The chambermaid thinks
How lovely she is
admiring her hair, and the cut
of her dress. Then wrinkles up her nose

and scurries off. *Georgina.*
This man beside her
in the *pince-nez*
is her husband. He etches their name
into the guest book
in perfect copper-plate while pulling off his cape.
Each flourish is controlled. *William
and Georgie.*

His mind's on other things. Poetry for one.
Iseult. The nature and the quantity of love.
A strange thing, surely. There's nothing
she can do. Instead,
nothing to lose,
she says
that she will write for him.

His eyes like a turning tide, a prophesy!

★

Her hand moves in silence
gliding like the coloured sands
of the egg timer her friend
brought back for her after a summer's day
on England's south-west coast. She kept it
in her pocket for a year
until it cracked and burst.
Her memories move, particle by particle,
to things she knows
she must not think about right now.
If only she could concentrate!
The colours in the sand!

She remembers the walk they took beside the ocean,
remembers how she wore her new galoshes
to disguise her ballerina feet. Country of rains,
betrayals, towers. The green bread
of her childhood. The smell of peat
and milky puddings.

★

She is worrying about her babies,
how they will grow
inside her so she learns to wear her body
like an out-grown dress,

wondering whether
when they're old enough
they'll have to fight
somebody else's war.
How much will it hurt?

A small voice echoes
in her head, telling her
it will always be this way. Anxieties. She wishes
she could banish them, let them
float out from her head for just one hour.

She remembers,
she remembers,
she remembers.

Like an itch, slowly and deliberately,
she scratches the page with her pen.
We have come to give you metaphors for poetry.

★

Tomorrow he will write
to friends, telling
of the easiness of marriage,
and when she wakes up from her dreams
she finds him
sleeping peacefully beside her.
Her hands cup
the cool dark sack between his legs.
How she loves him!
White sheets gleam in the moonlight
as she strokes his cheek,
brushing away the sprigs of sea-lavender
which sprout from his ears, from the tips
of his cowlick hair.

I Know Exactly the Kind of Woman
I'd Like to Fall in Love With

If I were a man.
And she would not be me, but
older and graver and sadder.
And her eyes would be kinder
and her breasts would be fuller;
the subtle movements
of her plum-coloured skirts
would be the spillings of a childhood summer.

She would speak six languages, none of them my own.
And I? I would not be a demanding lover.
My long fingers, with her permission,
would unravel her plaited hair.
And I'd ask her to dance for me occasionally,
half-dressed on the moon-pitted stairs.

Lovesong to Captain James T. Kirk

Captain. I never thought we'd come to this.
But things being what they are, being adults,
stardate '94, it's best to make the best of it
and laugh. What's done is done. Perhaps
I'll start to call you Jim or Jamie, James....

No one was more shocked than me when I arrived
(*the lady doth protest*) to find
my bruised and rainy planet disappeared
and me, materialised and reconstructed
on board the starship Enterprise, all '60s
with my lacquered beehive and my thigh-high
skirt in blue, my Dr Martens and my jeans
replaced by skin-tight boots and scratchy blue-black
nylons ripping up my less than perfect calves. Sulu
looked worried. Spock cocked one eyebrow
enigmatically, branding my existence
perfectly illogical. How nice, I thought, his ears.
Uhura smiled of course and fiddled
with her hair. *O James,*
truth is I loved you even as a child....

O slick-black-panted wanderer holding
your belly in, your phaser gun
on stun, and eyes like conference pears!
You're not my type, but I undress you
and we fuck, and I forgive
the pancake make-up and mascara,
the darker shadows painted round your eyes.
The lava lamp goes up and down. We're
a strange unison. Politically mismatched.
Our mutual friend the Doc takes notes.
Go easy, Bones! Scotty is beaming, and
shouts *Energise!* and all of a sudden you remind me

of my dad, my brother and my mum,
my body rising like a shadow from the past
on top of you. As I press your arms behind your head
I drape my breasts so that you brush
my nipples gently with your lips almost
involuntarily as we boldly go. Come slowly,
Captain, as we do, with both our pairs of eyes tight closed.

Loving the Greeks

Vos exemplaria Graeca
Nocturna versate manu, versate diurna
                   –Horace

Being girls, we thought it best to love the Greeks
sedately taught us in an attic schoolroom, the Latin master

with his legendary grin making us mistresses
of *the other language* as we heaved an aspirate

apostrophe right from our breathy souls
into the script of the *Lexicon Graecum*. The conjugation

of irregular verbs, the declension of an abstruse noun
came easily. Together we razed citadels, flamed triremes,

routed the barbarians bare-breasted, hand-in-hand,
lifting to glory the cunning of the Greeks. We were always

fast to learn, scorning the rhetoric of Cicero
for the travels of Herodotus; and being *outré*

Ovid's Book of Love, which was, by then,
allowed us, was considered "out" in favour

of the Sapphic fragments, an algebra of meaning
that relieved a frown of footnotes

with the touches of her seventh-century
(B.C.) inflammatory kiss. In mathematics

we also soared, almost in tears
at the arbitrary beauty of a chalked-up phrase

where meaning was a problem of another sort.
Let $\theta = \Pi\mu^2$!

How often I think of us together, now, being girls,
declining love, writing our lives in pictures,

arm-in-arm, with an old world
where it was more difficult

to find the perfect answer
to the he loves / she loves part of it.

Soap

The bouncer with the slashed face, they say he killed a man.
But still you dance
when he asks you to dance. You remind him

You couldn't knock a hole in Wednesday's wet Echo.
That bird on the telly, the tits on her.
But always you open the door for a lady.

The girl he says he's seeing,
she says he makes her safe.
We were cut up, of course, at the news –

the railway track, the noose.
You calling me a scally?
But we live with death and the pros

on Hope Street. Football's the thing.
In Liverpool we have *a lorra lorra laughs.*
I won't be held responsible if he goes free.

Now I ask you, princess, chasing dragons,
do woolly backs make better kissers?
Sinbad. Mother. Can a girl love a girl?

Why is it so hard to feel so close?
The body in the garden gets up and walks.
For a year he washed his hands until they bled.

Metamorphoses

No one believes I'm Marilyn Monroe, 36-28-36. At fifty,
5'10, a beard and thirteen stone, not even me. But you have to dream.
A girl can't help it. I think of her like nothing else:
her breasts, a strip of thigh. The way a body moves. *Love Goddess.*
Her teeth like buttons on an open shirt; her prawn-pink lips,
that mole. And her face like a white flower, blossoming, blossoming.
Her heels tap out my destiny, a sexy, breathy tune. I want
to step out from this body like a snake would lose its skin.

My shrink wears wigs and slacks. I wear a yellow dress,
have polish on my fingernails. She speaks in baritone,
butch to my *femme.* My legs cross at the ankle, hers the knee.
More of a man than me. I wanted a couch I could lie right back on.
A vase of lilies, or Egyptian artefacts. A way I could explain my-
self. My self. My. Self. Instead an upright chair. A large-spooled tape-machine.
The window ladling the sunlight like syrup from a tin. My eyes
a glass of water, shrinking on the window sill.

She made me watch the op, on video, the curtains drawn. Where
parts of me would go. Adjustments, hormones, sutures, scars. It changes
nips and tucks all right. The canopies of flesh. No going back. Making me
question everything. I cried. Considering myself in terms of pain. Just like
bereavement, moving house, divorce, or finding a new name. The endless
rearrangements. Three years later and I find (excuse the cliché, please)
I'm *falling in love again.* The woman I once married.
Her ordinary beauty makes me pale.

She says she loves me and she likes it. Hot. The little places
where I've learned to push my tongue. Her two hands brush my breasts
like angel wings, like tiny falling stars. Her mouth. The way
I feel it. Here. The space between us changes shape each night,
opens and closes, kaleidoscopic loops and whirls. Sometimes
Diamonds are a girl's best friend. You know? *Boop-boop-be-doop.* Our joke.
And *Happy Birthday,* Marilyn. Last night as perfect yet more perfect
than a wedding ring, our bodies rising, falling. There,
growing between us an exquisitely shaped O.

Shadowplay

I come to you like a child, as only an adult can,
with the silence
growing and shrinking.
These are the strange geographies of hurt.

You hold my head in your hands
as if it were a globe
rocking me slowly
from side to side. As if love
were a country difficult to place.
Now you smile, and this is enough to make me weep.

On the blank walls of the familiar room
your soft hands are intimate with shadows. Softly,
they surprise me,

making duck with an arch of wrist,
making wolf with a clasp of hands.
Fingers are beak, then snout and brow.
Those two familiar bitten thumbs
sprout up inquisitive as ears.

This is your way of playing forgiveness.
In these half-light moments
you are rabbit, monster, dove.

Later, I make bets on all the things you'll not create:
cash in on earthquakes, truth,
lose out on hope, desire,

your porcelain heart with its hairline fractures.

Blue

Noon in Greenwich Park. A freak heat wave.
We've take-out from Pistachios and all around
mothers and children spreading themselves out under the trees
and us, out to lunch. We are laughing about Frank O'Hara, Lancashire,
talking love, sex, time, in the hours before your train. I watch your
straight, white teeth, curious, your clean brown
hands. It feels like weeks ago. This morning
as I'm showering, the sun strikes me like a belly-dancer
and I smile, moving my hips against the soap.
My hair is only just drying as I buy groceries –
oranges and paracetamol – and it is 12:39 or 12:43
depending on what clock I check
when the car breaks down in the multi-storey.
When the AA man I've waited 50 minutes for says
You've got a silly name, I smile
for the second time that day. In dungarees
with oil on my hands and cheeks,
I'm feeling sexy and amazed. He starts the AX
with jump leads. That's quick, I say and he grins
writing 3 YEARS GARRANTY on a green slip
for a new battery. We don't hang about!
The car's dead heart on the grimy floor,
pink like a wound, replaced.
                                    Driving home
with the windows down
I think how many names there are –
inchoate — bougainvillea — love —
for not so many things.
And cooking supper for my lover sing him
choruses and highlights from *Fiddler on the Roof*.
A blessing on his head.
                                    Later
I cry for all my indiscretions.
                                    Remembering being 19,
reading Whitman and Moore
in the seminar room, the *yah honk*

of the wild goose, quavering. The steeple-jack,
the steeple's solid pointed star.
                        Tonight I'm balancing all this
in my head, watching the sky purple like a bruise
and thinking of you as I read *Time Out*
on Jarman's latest and most probably his last:
In the pandemonium of image
I present you with the universal blue.

And Please Do Not Presume

And please do not presume it was the way we planned it,
nor later say we might have tried harder,
or could have done better. Nor remind us of the things we didn't take –
the hints, the trains, the tonics,
the tape recordings of ourselves asleep,
the letters of a previous lover,
the photos of each other as a child.

And please do not presume our various ways of making up,
of telling lies and truths, the way we touched
or laughed, the Great Mistakes, the tiger suit,
our list of *Twenty Favourite Movie Classics*,
breakfast in bed, red wine, the different ways we tried
to make each other come
were anything else than the love we wanted

or that we did no more or less than anybody might have done.

And more, do not presume we could have stopped it –
like a clock, a gap, a leak, or rot — or made it
last much longer than it did,
or that the note on the fridge that one of us left
wasn't sweetly meant, but badly spelt.
Step One of Ten Proggressive Ways to Dissolution.

The Dinosaur Summer

That year, the filmmakers built dinosaurs,
with crops of tripods and gesticulations,
the double-stranded kick starts mapped
onto a blueprint of the Mesozoic, reconstructed,
pea-brained, and extravagant. *Apatosaurus ajax,*
Triceratops horridus. Appropriately Hollywood.

After prolonged castings it was rumoured
that the leading man went down with mumps,
the leading lady quietly disappeared.
And all the while ferocious debutantes, the dinosaurs,
emerged victoriously from behind the screen
of trees and backdrop trees. Each take became as painful

as the pulling of a hairy mammoth's tooth.
Nobody laughed. The dinosaurs were unresponsive,
chewed on papaya, fake arrowroot. Occasionally
they snarled, best side to camera, all their
computerized mechanics squeezed to anarchy
and camouflaged in beautifully-dyed skins.

Even the famous paleontologists were heard
to say they'd had it with their ancient temperaments
like babies. Squalling. The insufferable heat, they said,
was quite insufferable without their colleagues' wives.
For six long weeks we squabbled in the air-conditioned hum,
iced coffee Spanish style, ate, drank, breathed, lived

the Prehistoric. Then hardly said a word for weeks,
at last could only lie, deep-breathing anxiously
and side by side we barely touched except, I'm told,
in someone else's dreams. Impossibility
dawned with the morning, sank with the purpling
evening skies. One time, at dusk, after a shoot

cancelled due to seventeen freak minutes of white rain,
I found a footprint in the damp, bright earth
so large and real I thought that no one had invented it
and stretched inside it like a grave. When the rainy season came
for real the whole crew left. The director was a broken man,
was last heard jabbering a feeble *Cut!* in tears.

I remember how we laughed together then,
rolled on the floor, in stitches, clutched at our sides.
Each mad hypothesis about the dinosaurs' extinction
rang strangely true under their watchful eyes.
I remember how we saw the experts off, their silver trucks
grumbling into the middle distance as they waved,

whispering frantically between themselves that
the beginning of the dinosaurs was the beginning of the birds. How,
in the downpour, the curious, spiked jungle flowers,
the only foliage the dinosaurs despised, began to bloom
exquisitely, birthing the smell of paradise. I remember.
We surprised ourselves. Were suddenly aroused.

Summer

Summer is a lazy god, and all promises.
He says he will never leave,
was a long time coming
with swallows in his air –
petulant, weeping.

Waking early one morning
I watch him from the bedroom window,
barefoot on the wet grass,
stalking the garden and beside himself
with all the brilliant flowers.

With soft, dry hands, he soothes their heavy heads.
My children's books, too
that were carelessly left on the lawn all night

unread and ruined by the rain.

from *Signs Round a Dead Body* (1998)

What It's Like To Be Alive

after Django Bates

I remember the nights, and the sounds of the nights,
and the moon, and the clouds, then the clear sky

and the stars and the angels on the Rye;
and I remember the way we knelt on the bed, how the bedclothes
were a tide, and the sunlight was a tide, and how everything pulled,

and I remember the trains, leaving and arriving,
and I remember the tears, your tears and my tears

and how we were children, not lovers,
how the angels cried,

and I remember your face and your coming in my hands,
and the clouds, and the stars, and how, for a moment,
with our eyes tight closed how the planets lurched

and the angels smiled,
and I remember how I did not know if this was grief or love,

this hot pool,
and the sounds,
and then nothing –

a watermark held up to the light,
a boat rowed off the edge of the world.

Signs Round a Dead Body

Some day, by chance, you'll find that you're the first
to find the body of a man: as you walk one evening in an unknown wood,
or stroll along a secret beach – drunk or asleep ? –
enter a long familiar room
which has a silent staring body
at its corner or its end. Remember, then, that it's your duty to remember:

how the hand lay on the ground precisely, how the neck
was placed despairingly, the line of vertebrae,
a turn of ankle or a turn of head. If you've no camera
you must note exactly how his soft dark hair's
rained green with light or leaves.
Note how each toe is unresponsive when it's tickled,
by opening door, by rabbit, or sleepy tide; the way that
pine cones or novellas have been thoughtlessly
strewn round him – silent as himself, like meteors, unopened, gifts
like huge forgotten shells. And you must check
whether the ground or floor's disturbed or
trampled down, whether the leafy carpet's crumpled,
scarred with ash or trailed with blood.

Remember it's your duty to examine and write down
the smallest sign which may be vitally important.
Use your eyes! Be vigilant! Let nothing
be too small! And when you're finished, and you must return,

open the newspaper you found at some inconsequential place.
Sit for some time, and read, perhaps. Take three deep breaths.
If it is possible, drink tea. After a while follow the murmuring voices
and the faceless snores that are the other men,
whose sounds that strangely amplify at night
appear from nowhere like a thread.

The One that Got Away

In the Midleton factory
where you worked for three summers
you fell for a woman
you swore you would marry
if only for the sake
of the tale you could tell
years later
about the day when you met:
this doe-eyed, wide-hipped,
Inspectress of Peas, who

testing for sweetness, consistency,
size – this will kill you, you said –
with the Pea Tenderometer,
you made jump from her skin.
(Sweet Jesus, this your only sin,
to lean across her gently,
nibble at the darted cotton apron
covering her breasts
and whisper how you wanted her...)
And who, in fear, surprise

punched a perfect, pea-shaped hole
straight through your thumb.
These days, when you hold your hand
up to the light, squint through yourself
like a painter, with one eye open
and one eye closed
at all the aching sky
and start on this story
with a squeeze and a smile,

I'm still not sure.
The one that got away?
The pea-shaped flesh?
The pear-shaped girl?

The Fish

rainbow, rainbow, rainbow...
　　　　　　　　　　　　　–Elizabeth Bishop

I go to sleep with the taste of you, and this is not the first time
for you are too much with me. And these are your hands
in the darkness. This is the rough shape of
your face, only. Your hair, your ear, your thigh.
　　　　　And then, out of nowhere, your tongue like a hot little fish.
A blue fish, glinting electrics,
a fish accustomed to basking, I suppose,
in the clear, hot waters of some tropical isle.
Not an ordinary fish, not a fish I could haul from the waters,
or not easily. Not a fish accustomed to travelling in solitude,
but one used to a rainbow accompaniment,
one used to the sea's depths, and her sulky harbourings,
one used to the rockpools and the undertow, the colour of the sands.
And how suddenly you swam into me!
　　　　　And was it your mouth, or the memory of your mouth?
Or was it a fish? Whatever it was, it was there.
There in the bloodstream, bruising artery, vein,
as it swam, heading, no doubt, for the heart.
Then you stopped it
　　　　　and it basked in the blue pools of my elbow, where you
stroked it for a while;
then you asked it to dart, from my hips up my spine,
you asked it to wander to the tilt of my breastbone
where tickled like a salmon, it leapt,
　　　　　it leapt;
you asked it to journey from my shoulder to my neck, to the soft place
behind my ears
where you solemnly forbade it, asked it instead to
rest for a while, and then turn back
saying *Fish, fish, my brilliant fish*
and something I can't remember now
on the furthermost tip of my tongue, like a dream.

Sheep Piece

(i)

The Couple

Remember the photo the sheep took of us?
My face made tentative and ugly in the sun,

and you in the shirt that would have matched your eyes
except that you were (humbly?)

looking at the ground?
We couldn't understand a word she said,

but somehow as it came about, there was no need
for spoken promises or speeches, no need

for *Smile, please!* or a grudging,
teeth-clenched *Cheese!* In a sheepish way

we looked and locked so perfectly together –
my flowing bright blue skirt hitched up,

my shoelaces, my plaited hair, undone.
And I really can't remember why we got down on our knees

except we weren't quite able to believe
– who could? – in such a sudden, perfect

kind of love, or even in ourselves,
that summer, let alone the sheep,

the polaroid emerging,
and all the attendant angels fussing round.

(ii)

The Sheep

As if four legs were eternal condemnation
to a horizontal life! As if they'd never seen
a sheep before, gone vertical! They thought
I was a god, the tightened curls of my golden coat
shining and radiant. Not a rare breed,
badger-faced or speckled, just a local,
newly-washed and happy, afro-combed.
And yet it was as if I was about
to steal their souls, the way they looked at me,
so innocent, like children,
as they prayed there on the stubbly
sheep-chewed ground. And then another thing,
they were amazed I shared a language with them,
rated their technologies, could wield a Kodak
good as any other sheep. They blinked and
shuffled, finding I was eloquent, a little bossy,
charming, perspicacious, sometimes rude. But
proud of sheep-heritage, glad to be ruminant
and beardless, progressive, self-controlled...
(Ok, I was an amateur, but it was just
that moment that I wanted:
them making sheep's eyes
as the sun, glowing behind them,
slipped gently through the trees.)

(iii)

The Photograph

Funny how it starts. With an itch
when it's least expected. How it spreads
like a blush would, on a body of velvet,
a spreading soft discordance
edging slowly through the spectrum
until you are a shiny hard oasis
sucking all the colours in.
You have to make yourself remember
how you always start from scratch
before your features decompose
into dimensions, all
your plain white surface areas
confused. You have to tell yourself
it's only transient, until, like a chameleon,
you find you're doing it again,
with someone, something else –
being a woman, now, and smaller
than she'd thought, and younger,
a man quite boyish and wild-haired.
That's when you start to hurt,
feeling the strain of everything contained,
each particle, each colour. You're not
yourself, the photographic paper, or
the thing you photographed,
the lovers or the landscape;
not the moment when you stole them, either,
all that bemusement, and contentment,
all those colours, all that joy,
ventriloquized imperfectly, so perfectly.
Flesh-coloured flesh. The girl, the boy.

Making Out

Now it was airports that she needed –
to sit there going nowhere
counting aeroplanes like sheep,

with Concorde like an archaeopteryx or angel
and Egypt, Russia, the Azores and Lithuania
spinning in her head. She'd sit there

writing letters that she knew she wouldn't send,
telling him about the dull, red moon, the way
the landscape then, so pale, unreal,

the fishermen, the midnight seas
had been tattooed like hieroglyphs
in blues and golds

deep into her skin. It was his hands, I think,
she could imagine best
travelling across her. But she thought about the way

he'd kiss her too, the way she'd smile, nod yes
to his demolishing her. The way he'd start
to reassemble, slowly, in the rented bed

her mouth, her throat, her shoulders, breasts,
her knees, her arms, her thighs, her calves, and love etc.

From His Coy Mistress

Some days I think I will become a nun,
book in a convent miles away,
cut off my hair, and dress in black
wanting to purge myself of men.

I'd kneel and pray and chant a lot,
lie in a narrow bed,
devising titles of unwritten books:
A Semiotics of Flirtation. Love:
Some Concepts of the Verb, "To Sin".

One thing's for sure. By wanting you
I'm not the woman that I think I am.
I cannot eat or sleep at all,
just think about your lovely mouth

the eerie moonlight and the Northern seas.
And hope my body's still the temple
that you'd come upon, by chance,
to excavate a hundred years from now,

burn incense in, and dance and sing,
oh yes, and weeping, worship in.

An Indian Summer

Sometimes it's as if we're lost,
a place on a map that no one can find.
And I have to invent us, over and over,
give us names that we smile at:
Nova Nostalgia, Valentine Corner, Lost Love's Grove.
O my soft and freckled river!
I'm the Edwardian lady in an unmanned boat
lying on cushions, with the sun on her face
lazily trailing one ungloved hand.

Song of Despair

Emerge tu recuerdo de la noche en que estoy.
El rio anuda al mar su lamento obstinado

Abandonado como los muelles en el alba,
Es la hora de partir, oh abandonado.
                                        –Neruda, "Songs of Despair"

If I made a snow man to remember you,
a sharp-edged ghost, a little god, to better understand you,
if I gave it eyes, a nose, a small set mouth,

if I smiled, and flirted, licked its modelled ear,
or its icy cheek till my tongue was a flame
would it come to life,

its moulded shoulders and its wooden limbs?
Would its frozen heart
grant me a wish?

Would it dissolve in a flurry as the winds blew over it?
Would it melt,
so that matter transformed,

so that water,
a muddied pool,
would be all that was left?

So that
as I knelt
I could raise you

as if from the dead
to my dried and emptied mouth.
And would the earth still be frozen?

Frozen.
My footprints in the white fields of Tartarus,
crows-feet, laughter, feathers-in-the-snow.

45

★

I have sent you away.
I have sent you to where sky meets sea
to the silence   where the sea

imagines itself;

to the sky,
                                which overcomes us,
being itself and nothing,
                  simply.

Without purpose, with derision, I have sent you away.
I have sent you drunken, into the dark,
weighed down with weightlessness.
I have sent you, like an angel fallen from the heavens.
I have wished you lonely, hated and bemused.
I have sent you drunken, into the dark.
I have sent you hatred like a glowing wreath.

I have sent you bitterly, into the dark.
It's there love, only,
                  that you'll meet me.

★

I said,
make me unfaithful as I sleep.
Make me unfaithful waking me from sleep.
I said, let me give you this thing, I said

furnish me
with this small, hard thing,
Bring me oranges, pomegranates, starfruit.
Bring me mangoes, kumquats, pears.

And make me discover you
as you do.
And how could I blame you for that?
Or my own stink in that stinking room
with flowers strewn on that hard square bed &
amethysts in my ears.

★

When I found you, or, as the story goes,
when you found me;

when you took my hand and walked beside the sea,
or refused to take my hand as we wandered through the hills,

or when undressed, I was too scared to face you,
or when you looked askance at me and didn't smile

I didn't know if it was love
or if love itself was a cure or a disease –

that thing we cannot really name or see,
know only symptoms of.

★

So I raised you from the dead.
So I washed you, licked your armpits, the soles of your feet, untangled
the spidery lines of your matted hair,
picked leaves and insects from your well-shaped limbs,
blew life into your mouth
and sang to you.
So I suckled, promised, fed and enfolded you.
So I hated, loved, scorned even myself,
was tenderness, a body to you.

And the world was ours,
for you were risen from the dead.

And when you had loved enough.
When you had loved me till love was not even enough;
when you had tied, hurt, salvaged me,
when you had shaved off every hair on your body, as a gift;
when you had carved my name, a scar
on your forearm
I sent you,

back to the dead,
kicked the soft earth in your sweet mouth
and left you to the dogs, the emptiness, the hillside
of your own self

which even now, in its horror, surprises me.

★

So maybe I will say that I am lost –
that my heart is lost, or that I've lost my heart;
and ghosts, like the memory of water
cannot be dissuaded,
surface from the newly-fallen snow.

So maybe I will say,
squatting against the coolness of a wall
or sleeping on a boat, a transatlantic plane,
that there is nothing left for me to do.
This loving has become a life.
And this is the process of staying alive,
knowing that you will not come.

★

When I say that your shoulders are an ox's, strong and unlovely,
when I say that your belly and its deeply-set umbilicus
mean nothing,
when I say that the pits of your eyes beneath their brows, myopic
are uncared for,
when I say that the roughness of your cheek,
the unseemly length between nose and lip,
that your elliptical smile
or that the noise you make in sleep,
your farts, grumbles, dream-debris,
remind me of a dog
or that the tilt of your head, or the crossing of your leg
your bearing, in fact,
simply is not beautiful

it is the same as when I take the oath to testify
I do not love you.

It's the same as when I promise faithfully
that every word I've ever said is true.

★

Tonight the trees are heavy with snow,
so remote and yet so touchable.
I could stand here forever, I suppose,
watching the street in the streetlight
stiffen like a corpse, a freshly-laundered uniform.

And I could bring you words
but my lips are frozen, and my tongue is numb.
I could bring you a coffin to bury the words.
I could bring an assemblage of bones –
hair, particle, living matter –
to question the lack in me, in love.
I could bring the pain between men and women.
I could bring the cold air and the subway and the river,
all the city's sounds.
I could bring you love in a glass of water,
in a touch, in a word.
I could bring you everything, except delight

to blow you open.
I could not bring the blizzard or the storm,

only myself, only love,
my own taste, my own smell,

your mouth as my own
as I lean into you

mingling the startled syntax of our clothes.

★

When you undress me, and you will –
in ten years, or in twenty

and my greyed hair blows heavily
across your shoulders like a sail;

when I am the spring tide and neaps,
                the high tide about you;
when I'm like a boom, switching in the breeze
or lolling against you, that lone, forgotten oar,
when you come to know again my mast,
my helm, my creaking decks
when you relearn the names
by which to call me
know me port, fo'c'sle, starboard, bow and stern,
and I am the boat
in which you sail home to greet me

remember me as I was
and the first time we set out to sea, and see
now the scar on my breast
a starry bullet

where, as I leapt and soared,
with foam in my hair on that tiny raft
thoughtlessly as a smile,
an illegible glance
you looked up,
           crowing,
                 shot me.

Song for Winter

These days, even love is terrible:
like a plane, taking off inside the heart.
And now there's nowhere left to go,
for you've brought me to the edges of hell
with your soft ways and your gardener's hands;
you, who'd turn your hand, your eye, to anything,
filling the house with the smell of bread and roasting lamb,
bringing in wood for fire from the yard
as if it were a task of love, or something to be guilty of....
And if I cried out in the night, if you cried too,
to the buildings and the lightless houses,
to trucks, to retail parks, to helicopters, taxis,
the digital, the car alarms, who is there to answer?
Who, amidst the landscape that I almost recognise
the rest homes and the hospitals, the pubs,
the restaurants, the neoned clubs, the bric-à-brac
of roof and trees, a mutilated statue in the park,
who laughing, who retching, who weeping
who is there to tell how sorrow puts a name to sorrow
with language or the body? TV, the radio,
the little gods of noise? For we carry love
like a kind of pain: desire like terror,
a sticklebacked wave... and who, looking down,
would offer more than this, a shrug, a look of pity, or a smile?
Who, seeing us now, our gaze upturned, the knowing stars
like a litter of rice, confetti, fractured bone or broken glass
could pluck us, unhurt from the universe,
rechart the stars, make everything strange?
What's more, who'd even ask, or have the right to ask
why nothing comes of nothing, still?
I play back voices on the answerphone, a prayer.
Tree-twist   feather   tangle-hair.

Song for the Absence of Her Lover's Voice

(i)

A bright day that might be brighter with you here.
I think about the way that time can fill itself,
how space is dark and replicates until it makes me hurt;
how words, making themselves from nothing, too
are all this distance lets us share.

Your presence, meanwhile, like a rhyme, can take me to a corner
by the hands, and,
so quietly, my love, so beautifully,
knows just the way to keep me there.

(ii)

When in our March, our April and our June
we saw a bird, an animal
that no one knew the name of
we were quiet. The winter came and disappeared too soon.

This silence I remember now. Also the gaps, the breath,
my mouth, the noises that I make.
How after seven days without you I am lost.
On the telephone, a hundred miles away, you tell me all of this.
Quite unashamed, I steal your poem like I'd steal a kiss.

Song for Rain

I want the rain to be in everything.
Not a season or an afternoon, but rain in everything:
a clean, blue, repetitious life.

I want it in fires, gorse fires by the sea, candles that we love by;
when you are drunk, fearful, I want it in dreams,
in feathers, small stones, whole forests of green.

I want it there in the night when you shout and sweat
when nothing will comfort you.
When I take your arm,

when I shake my head with sheer joy like a dog
and the silence is sudden, beautiful, forgiving.
I want the rain to be terrible

in my eyes, in my hair.
And I want it in rivers, in stars, its sound, very simply,
familiar among the leaves and rattling windows

together when we wake.
I want it in wars, and the memory of words,
in pity and fear.

I want it, and you, and the rain, and not her, writing herself
all over your face.

Midnight Beach at Sizewell B

How ordinary it is,
like a shoebox, or a series of shoeboxes,
as if you could assemble it yourself,
make the dome complete, for instance, in a trice,
splitting two straight lines in half
then bending them
till they become two softly touching arcs
made pale and oddly solid,
silvered in a moment,
a gasp of breath on glass.
Yet still it would be nothing more than ordinary –
in fact it's this you can accept it for –
the line of cars, the lights, its gently low-key whirr,
the men and women on their shift
now laughing, muttering, perhaps, while
diligently clocking on; one tiny, smoking chimney
straying in the starless sky
as if all human error, pain
was quietly taken care of, here,
bundled up, smoothed out, and trimmed
catapulted centuries away.

A Brief Inventory of Facts about Snow

For months now, I've dreamed of nothing but snow,
how the six-sided crystals which descend on us *ex machina*
make an underworld of everything
so that waking in the warmth of orange,
staring through the window at the whitened skies
I want to go no further, want to fall back simply
in a drift of sleep, naming its colours, inconsistencies.
I want to ask the whole world what it makes of snow –
snow yellowed, or purpled, snow trampled or pristine,
how we remember or remember we've imagined it
or when we think we've first encountered it,
snow mounting on snow.
              From Scotland Sally laughs that Andrew,
feverish with flu, now dreams of going to work on skis.
And I imagine this tall man and the empty bed
as if he'd jumped from the window there and then
leaving a trail of parallel lines,
his white sheets like a rush of wings,
his hair like a halo as it streams
gold on white on blue.
              And Julia imagines mountains in a children's book,
snow like chocolate sauce on white ice cream,
a monochrome version in reverse, while Michael
shows me exactly how
to save my life in case of avalanche,
launching me upwards through the cold,
swimming a vertical length of snow.
              Alison, telling me to be happy, adds, in passing,
how Breughel, dissatisfied with images
of families, workers, friends
going about their daily business in the heat,
repainted canvases to make them winter
painting the joy of nothing into summer
as if, with snow itself,
he could, by trapping air between the flakes
now insulate the heat between the years

making plants survive, or people even,
making absence itself
                    complete.
And I remember April, fifteen years ago,
how Nicola swung on the blossoming tree
making the whole world blush.
How this, in its gentleness, in its surprise
was somehow too a vision of snow.
And Moss writes last,
smiling his way through careful inks
to tell me the tale of a William Bentley,
born Jericho, Vermont, and how he spent
his whole life taking photographs of snow,
proving beneath the microscope, each flake
as asymmetrical as women's breasts.
And all these words become a kind of rhapsody
on the way that snow transforms itself
as I curl up daydreaming, my knees pulled to my chest,
falling asleep with an unread book,
thinking yes, yes, I have to agree,
That's the glory, that's the wonder of snow.

Snow Song

All summer I've waited,
weaving this cloth of burrs and nettles
till my hands prickle and blister
like bubbles of oxygen
trapped under glass.

Then suddenly the snow:
snow being born of itself,
snow feathering your cheeks, lashes, lips,
snow being more than itself,
the colour of nothing. Snow
like the wings of a long-necked bird....

And I call you, whispering:
A few days is all we have.

Calcium

Because I love the very bones of you
and you are somehow rooted in my bone
I'll tell you of the seven years

by which the skeleton renews itself
so that we have the chance to be
a person, now and then, who's

something other than ourselves;
and how the body, if deficient,
will bleed the calcium it needs –

for heart, for liver, spleen –
from bone, which incidentally
I might add, is not the thorough

structure that you might
suppose, but living tissue which
the doctors say a woman of my age

should nurture mindfully with fruit,
weight-bearing exercise, and supplements
to halt the dangers of a fracture when I'm old.

And because I love you I will also tell
how stripped of skin the papery bone
is worthy of inscription, could hold

a detailed record of a navy or a store of grain
and how, if it's preserved
according to the pharaohs,

wrapped in bandages of coca leaf, tobacco,
it will survive long after all our books
and even words are weightless;

and perhaps because the heaviness of your head,
the way I love the slow, sweet sense of you,
the easiness by which you're stilled,

how the fleshy structures that your skeleton,
your skull maintain, are easily interrogated,
it reminds me how our hands

clasped for a moment, now, amount
to everything I have; how even your smile
as it breaks mc up, has the quality of ice,

the long lines of loneliness
like a lifetime ploughed across a palm,
the permanence of snow.

My Father's Hair

For it has stood up like a coxcomb before a fight.
For it is whiter than lace on a bobbin or snow on a bough.
For in his youth it was auburn, leading to blackness.
For it has a grave insouciance,
what they call in Sassoon's a natural air.
For it has resisted gels and lotions, brilliantine, mousses.
For it has been photographed, ridiculed, admired, swept back.
For it speaks the language of wild things, everywhere.
For it has suffered the Barbary of barbers, and my mother.
For it has been tamed with deerstalkers, baseball and camouflage caps.
For it is something of a pirate or an admiral.
It is a spark transmitter and a special constable,
it is harrier, jumpjet, parachute, chinook.
For it is salt on an eyelash, fresh from the sea.
For it is loved by many women of the district
and is piped aboard the sternest of vessels.
For it cannot be mentioned, the pot of Vitalis
she gave him on their honeymoon.
For its mind is as fast as light, the elastic stretch
of a falling star. It is not anybody's servant.
For we will say nothing of Delilah and Seville.
It is both gravel path and skating rink.
It is velvet, it is epaulettes. It is sunrise, it is sunset.
O my father's hair! It is an unsung hero!
But because of the sickness, or the cure for the sickness,
it lies like an angel's on the pillow:
long white strands, like wings, or long white wings, like hair.

Atlantis

for my parents

I try to imagine you dead
caught now in this moment of love
as if trapped spectacularly in a lava flow
and sunk beneath the waves –
just now, as you hold each other,
arm resting on waist or thigh,
lip resting on lip;

and I try to imagine myself
grown suddenly old
at the point of your dying
at this moment when I see how love begins,
becomes itself again;
and when that tenderness

again becomes desire
so that your children's children's
children, in a look, a word, perhaps,
an errant vowel, might find you
somehow by mistake,
an ice-blue underwater city

suddenly come across.

Spells

(i)

The bed becomes a page, the white sheets
where we leave ourselves,
hair, fluids, sloughed-off skin,
cells of the self grown out of themselves
not living but unchanged, as any lover's history.
And here, like a wing, or a sycamore seed
is the L of my arm and here is my hand
on your halo of hair. I want to spell out all
the harboured messages of joy, make an alphabet
of our hands and bodies, rewrite our movements
make everything strange. To speak what is us
what is you, or me, each vowel, each consonant
now coded in the silent movements of our sleep.

(ii)

The vowels, the consonants of speech, sound wrong
because like all translators we have failed. We learn to misread
or adequately speak, the words that waltz, cavort or slip
terrible, on the starry page. Instead we're left with all the painful
ghostings of ourselves. *Her voice* in another language, the way you say
his eyes. And words as unaccountable to things as love.
And memories slither. And thoughts collide.
When we dream it is ice that we dream of, and snow.
When you say that you love me, you say it in sleep.
We're all of us dying, but I want this to live.
Our days collapse, the nights draw in. A smudge of mouth,
a flurry of hands. Even the darkness is crying out
through the pale O of your dreaming mouth.

(iii)

Your soft mouth says my name,
makes me unfamiliar, makes me look at myself
from a distance again. But
the soft V of my breasts that I find
when at last you take hold of me, puts me to flight.
And this flight's still a bird's or an echo of bird
as softly I push into you, feathering your eyelids
with my tongue, strobing a cool, sandpapery cheek.
And when I write of myself
it is now as a 2, our joined lives
make the shape of a swan. *What makes us afraid?*
Beside us in the emerald water
the swan's white reflection.

(iv)

Your long body is a history I find a way to read,
negotiating bends and swan-like corners,
the map of constellations on your back, the isthmus
of your ankle, the wayward hill of your contoured chest,
peaks of your buttocks, lovely knees.
I try to read you backwards, frontways
from top to bottom, right to left. I whisper in morse
to colour your dreams, then signal my errors,
eight semaphore Es. And if love is a mirror I see
only your face. And if love is a window I tap at the glass.
If I licked you alive would the whole summer warm me?
My sighs are spells, they are gasps for breath. The question mark
of your loving body rousing me at last to speech.

The Policeman's Daughter

after Paula Rego

When I see her there, shining her daddy's boots, the moonlight making the sky
a deep improper blue, I want to fill the night with stars, with rain,

I want for there to be a kind of stillness that as yet she can't contain
between the silent walls, the kitten's mew, and all the strange geometries of sleep

that in her task she will refuse. O, to heap words on her, flowers! suitors!
anything to take away the look of studied pain, to unravel

that moonsoaked mane, to make her someone ordinary who
suffers for a while, who doesn't keep her father wedged so deep

against her heart she hasn't anything but this to do:
to scrub and polish, rub and spit, each night at it again,

as if this making of her hand a hoof, making the leather strain
against her fingers, *so*, would always be enough, would heap

like a backwards prayer, scorn on her enemies, keep
sweet the properties of life, make something new

from nothing – the point where land meets sky
and's not itself or anything;

which is like love, where we begin.

from *Quiver* (2004)

For God mingles not with man; but through Love
all the intercourse and converse of god with man,
whether awake or asleep, is carried on.
　　　　　　　　–Plato, *Symposium,* "The Nature and Origin of Love"

I

The Cemetery

I've learnt to run, like an adult learns to sing,
the arpeggios of the body's muscles,
the biomechanics of the human scale,
forcing a life to be suddenly spoken,
a finger pressed to an ivory key, a note that issues
from an opened mouth, as if God or the gods
were already there, endorphins pulsing through
                                    the system,
the body's flux when contained in movement,
your hard-earned place in the world
on hold; I've learnt to take tarmac under my shoe,
to feel the spark between muscle and sinew
pushing the globe on its tilted axis,
the rib cage and its nesting heart,
ventricular walls and the pump of oxygen,
the flexion-extension of shoulder and arm
as you travel through light and a briskness of shadow,
suddenly animal, curious, terrible,
just for a moment never-grown old....

It's the cemetery I run through now,
the snow-littered pathways of ordered mayhem,
the furnishings of its strange allotment,
recording angels, bears, dogs, gnomes,
a broken vase, a fading wreath, a votive candle
snow's snuffed out, Our Lady of Suburbia,
a rosary entwined in sculpted fingers,
propped beside a smiling buddha, a paper blue
chrysanthemum wilting in his hand.

Yet, through the wreckage of doggerel,
on marble, on granite, through the hum of cars
on the circling road, through the cool swathes of air
on this mist-hung morning,

a blackbird opens its feathery throat
pulling the sky and the skyline closer
so hedgerow and barbed wire and railing,
the crunch of my footsteps on glistening paths,
rise up together, clash and unite,

when suddenly I stumble, hit the ground,
become myself stretched out among the graves,
the frost, a plot of orange dirt. Slumped beside me,
shouldered by a gravestone,
ice keeping death alive, a woman's ruined body,
pierced with an arrow like a fallen bird.
What is it like to know death so slowly,
hair and fingernails still growing
like Lizzie Siddal's in the grave?
What is it like – the presence of absence –
the space you keep in that clenched right hand?

It's a body I know from snapshots, old albums
carrying histories, other lives, other selves.
William and Mara. Mara and Will.
There at the mouth, carved like a seraph's,
a dash, a dart, an outpost of blood.
Her eyes are ash-pits in saintly expression
like Christ's on the cross in an incense-fuelled church,
or that woman of sorrows – the mother, the lover –?
a flash like lightning in her crow-dark hair.

I think of her now, the twist of flesh
on her stripped, lean torso, remember a smile,
a forthright look. I pick myself up
and my stomach retches;
I dizzy, double over, then throw up.
The movie I'm in is in black and white.
I note an absence of birdsong, the moan of the thaw.
Then the soundtrack arrests.
Was I wrong then, I wonder, remembering this:
how a voice from on high chastens us, comforts us?

Everything's still.

Underworld

Two policemen ferry me home.
I'm adrift in silence, a migraine of lights.
There's blood in my mouth, a taste of metal

like a coin placed under my tongue.

The Story of a Life

Will's home already, the dinner's on
as the house takes on his print.
I see him through the window,
gathering the light in shadows,
sitting with a cup, I guess,
of camomile and limeflower,
Bird playing as he reads his book.
Time swings back and forth
as evening is exposed.
Our ancestors collude in corners.
My grandparents from Bethesda, Liverpool.
His grandfather from Tipperary,
grandmother from Guangzhou.
I see them speaking Welsh/Chinese
and sipping Guinness in a brilliant pagoda.
Two dragons – east and west – collide.
And though I've phoned to say I'm late,
how will it be when he smiles, looks up
from the stories of Sui Sin Far,
when he says, "Listen to the story
of *My Chinese Husband*",
the month-old baby with his newly-shaved head;
or begins to tell me of his day at the hospital,
a woman with five foetuses inside her
they think they'll bring to term,
the woman he's been treating for three years
still waiting for a sperm, an egg;
how will it be when
I have to tell him,
when this narrative arrests
and the past opens
and time wobbles
and what I have to tell
becomes at once too long, too short?

Flashback

How does a photograph become a memory?
This one's not even mine, but I remember
Mara, grave as a kore, her sweater sleeves rolled.

How can I feel it, even now? The look on her face
as she guts a pair of rainbow trout;
in one swift action removes each head,

cleaving a knife that glints like quicksilver
dull against the papery bone.

Sky Canoe

I see, not feel, how beautiful they are.
                                    –S.T.C.

Sometimes this bed without love, this
settling to sleep like children,
hand-in-hand, knees fitted into knees,
the radio on low, our books, clothes,
daily lives strewn carelessly about the floor

is both more and less than I can bear.
Take this sky the night has given us –
not the Pleiades or the Seven Sisters,
Cassiopeia with her train of hair –
but a heaven we have made ourselves,
the bright planets of our bedroom firmament

glow-in-the-dark plastic stars
fixed to a painted square.

Arrangements

We've no idea whether to bury her or send her to the flames.
Next of kin, Will settles on a pale oak box, and
like a wedding dress the length of it,
a sheath of snow-white flowers.

My Husband, Will

I've loved him for seven years, loved him
in a way that means I always want to look.

It's something in the eyes,
the way that beauty wanders slowly into you

even now, as he sits there in his shirtsleeves,
his shoulders slightly hunched

against the darkness, as he slips into his book.
So why do I see them as I do,

there in a pause as the past drapes round us,
his hand a compass, her spine a map,

or as children, now, playing hopscotch or tag,
as her dark eyes flash – are they touching tongues? –

and he drapes his arm about her neck.
When I look in the mirror it is her face

not mine. The weight of the coffin on Will's shoulder
hurts me like the weight of love.

The Funeral

I hardly know anybody here.
Some friends of Will I nod to:
a white-haired man,
a blonde in black whose beauty is too telling,
a group of Goths, their make-up running.

Someone in a creased grey suit
reads a passage from the Bible
which, of course, I recognise:

Ecclesiastes VII.iii

When Will sits slowly, heavily beside me,
his head is bowed. We're holding a space
like life between us. The congregation murmurs, kneels,
becomes a row of question marks interrogating darkness,
a shaft of sudden light.

Block

I'd taken leave on Will's advice;
taken a year to remember myself,
left the university, philosophers,
taken time for the body, and simpler thoughts.
What use is a poet who doesn't write?
And for a while, it helped,
those blue and yellow pills like magic beans:
nothingness trapped like a leaf in amber,
sunshine pouring out.

Tail

He's watched me for two days, this plainclothes policeman
with uncertain eyes, a paunch, a greying crop:

he's familiar, now, with that over-the-shoulder, don't-
hurt-me look, the way I throw it to the middle distance,

unaware, on visits to the library, friends,
how space between us now is documented, marked.

He marvels at my knack of disappearing into doors,
how with a half-turn of the head

I can transform the everyday so swiftly,
silk handkerchiefs pulled from a folded palm,

a dove emerging from a hat. The outline of my frame,
now scattered in a mist of dust and light,

reminds him of the fingerprints he took, rolling each finger
across the page; fingers, he saw, still stained with ink

sitting beside me in the church to send the body off.
And my black Nissan

is quiet as a hearse, neither ghost nor echo,
the stretch of my shadow his only hope

as he follows me like a train of thought
through light-slicked, empty streets.

A Change in the Weather

Green shoots spike the frost
like secrets, promises that haunt us.
The sky is a mirror for space and light.
Yet something's not right.
Leaves fall in springtime like waterless koi,
unwanted gifts of exotic fruit.

Wonderland

Those wonder pills, their chemistry of light,
still keep me in a funny place,
as Erica, my oldest friend,
brings tea in willow-pattern cups,
her pregnant belly eight months heavy,
her hair a corona of auburn curls.

I feel like Alice in her flooded house.

At every corner now, or so it seems, is Mara's face,
a Cheshire Cat which grins and disappears.

And no one has the words I need,
till Erica, with a look I read
as either faith or doubt, her baby daughter
uncannily like her, curled up on her knees,
sends me home with a kiss, an unreadable smile:

"Pick up your pen and write."

Ghosts

The dead are with us still
however we love or lose them.
Where do they live, the ghosts we try to kill?
The dead are with us. Still
they wear us as they will,
sing us like a nursery rhyme, a hymn,
make something inside us irretrievably small
however we love or lose them

Ash Wednesday

I'm in the Bluebird driving home
as morning finds itself in clear, white skies,

the mass at St Nick's at the Pier Head failing me, finding
no place in me for words of faith,

just a sharp space in my upturned heart that might
be anywhere: a small white cup, a shattered vase,

when there, at the lights I swear I see her:
her straight body, those even shoulders,

combat trousers, a ballerina cardigan in grey,
her hair wound up in a silver dragon clip,

gold flashes, like wings, on brilliant white Nike.
As the lights change I count to ten,

turn the nearest corner, look again.
Of course, she's disappeared,

then I glimpse the dog
tethered to a railing near the top end

of the street. "Wait!" and I call her name.
But as soon as she's there, she's gone,

part *bandolero*, part *bas bleu*.
And all I have left is my dumb reflection,

the blurt of horns, the misted windscreen,
ash on my forehead, tears on my cheeks.

Liverpool Blues

The skyline in the moonlight, the river running thin,
my lover weeping lotus blossom for his next of kin.
The stars will tell their stories over Birkenhead and Camell Laird's.

In Berry Street, in Bold Street, in Princes Park and Princess Street
I've seen a girl I never knew and never thought to meet.
The Liver Birds have flown away, the cathedrals' doors are closed.

In hospitals and factories, bars, clubs, churches, loony bins,
something is uneasy beneath the city's restless din.
A woman has been murdered, yet no one says a word.

The homeless and the helpless, the workers on the street
have nothing left to live for, can only smell defeat.
My husband's left his heart elsewhere, my love has been foreclosed.

We're living in a borderland, somewhere between life and death,
losing ourselves in the search for a self.
It's a country of our making, the cards are curiously dealt.

The helicopter spotlights buzz us, lights come flooding in,
even our bedroom's no longer safe, we're living on a pin.
We mouth our dreams in the telling dark, but nothing can be heard.

We mouth our dreams in the telling dark, but nothing can be heard.
We mouth our dreams in the telling dark, and only words are lost.
We mouth our dreams in the telling dark, still nothing can be heard.

Good Cop, Bad Cop

They must practise their clichés till they know them by heart,
say their lines with this look as they play their part.
One drinks coffee with a dash of cold water.
And the one I've met before,
his firm hand cool at my greeting,
refuses to drink anything at all.

TIME OF DEATH.
CAUSE OF DEATH.
Found with the body, this:
a bundle of hand-written papers – poems? –
a bunch of unmarked keys.

Bad cop slams them on the table.

I'm meant to answer questions.

Good cop swills the dregs of coffee cooling, refuses to
                                        look up.

I recognise the keys as Will's, the writing as my own.

Quiver

Let's start with the stag.
No hedging, no prevarication,
no semiotics or white lies.
Let's start, simply, with this tale of transformation.
Artemis and Actaeon. As good as any other.
I'll begin by simply asking you,
Imagine this! *The weight of the antlers,*
the stagginess of the moulting coat;
the staggy eyes with their bushy lashes,
the intimacy of the moment
when for the first time
a man sees the body of a woman.
And then this man becomes a stag.
Let's start with the Dewars poster on the wall,
his proud glance, let's start
with the head at the feet of the huntsman,
the stag's blood, his rite of passage
daubed on his skin as if accidents with a razor
– the cheek-torn, cotton-woolly kind –
were all it took to make a man of him.
Let's start with what he once was
that day as he peeked and pried,
a young man, bold as brass,
in those days when seeing was doing,
the eucalyptus whispering
as this woman undresses
who is also a god. And while he watches her,
as water somehow possesses her,
rids the privacy of her well-formed body,
then gives itself up
like the body gives up perfume, sweat,
revealing her, as she emerges
clavicle, breast-bone,
the blue vein at her child-free nipple,
the thatch of hair that covers the pubis:
Artemis, single-minded,
casting about red-cheeked,

groping for her bow and arrow
refusing to be naked for this man.
That's when the story starts
in the terrible comedy of shame.
And when we ask how desire runs –
upwards on the spine's ladder, to the nape,
and down again
on that central point
between labia and the coccyx,
that private space the huntsman longed for,
perhaps wanted to bring
between thumb and forefingers
to know in himself interior joy –
we must ask then why desire that runs
between humans and gods
is always ill-fated as our story now
hangs on a breath, as we pin back our ears,
cut the umbilicus, its glistening thread....
Take Semele, consumed by fire
in the face of Zeus, Dionysus her son
left to mature on the incubator of
his father's thigh, a scrawny cry
as he was born, wriggling
from his tight papoose; or that bright nymph
Echo, known for her poetry, heartbreaking songs,
damned by Hera till her bones turned to stone
and her voice a whisper; Narcissus her lover,
condemned to keep looking,
transformed to a lonesome waterside flower....
But let's shift back our focus
to Actaeon/Artemis, and the goddess's companion
who had also spotted our peeping Tom,
who longed to push her breasts against his back,
rub peplon and chiton against that chest
for whom chastity is a spiritual heist,
who covets most the watermark streaks,
stretchmarks on a mother's skin,
who in Titian's painting failed again
under the skull of a stag. Faith,
let's call her that, who wanted nothing more

than the spillage of silver,
who as she watched him watching them
as they undressed, slipped off her dress,
this time without caution,
holding her arms above her head,
prolonging the moment of her nudity,
airing the flex and tautness of her limbs,
the narrow triangle of her unmarked back,
the downy base of that fragile neck.
Let's imagine what would have happened
had Artemis not spotted him.
For here it was, dark as a plum,
the genesis of a ruined moment,
the intoxication of a bird's first flight,
the rumination of the world,
a man aspiring to see the goddess,
and wanting what? To feel her goodness
not a violation; and a woman,
not a goddess, but infused with her goodness,
wanting to find a part of herself, in this man
as she felt his body as a line of pleasure:
it is done, here it is, we have done it, it is done.
For what she wanted was belief in a self.
What she wanted was to look at the goddess
to see something there of herself, too;
what she wanted
was to look at the man without fear and shame
with an image of herself with which to begin.
But that bronzed creature, which is where,
in a fashion, we began,
was no answer, as she peered into the bathing pool,
seeing the stag by her own face,
pregnant now, though she doesn't know it,
and the stag ripped apart by the hounds....
Those hounds! Imagined now as what?
An ever-changing line of mothers, daughters, long-lived women?
Antigone and Clytemnestra, Penelope and Joan.
The names might go on, being all things and nothing,
finding within themselves routes to becoming:
lovers of women, lovers of men. Names

trip off the tongue: Millicent, Sylvia,
Christabel, Emily, Angel Virginia, Non-nonsense Simone,
Glorious Gloria, Unblushing Germaine;
Fierce Luce, Brave Julia, La belle Hélène.
They burn like a catechism, are worthy of praise.
Here's hound Catherine, now, with her crown of thorns,
Little Saint Bride with her cow-print jacket,
Agnes the Borzoi, the Windhound Poor Clare.
Here's Sappho, Felicia, Aphra, Christina,
so many Elizabeths they can't all be named.
But let us return now to Faith,
the mother perhaps of all invention,
tears pouring from her virgin cheeks,
still hoping to find herself, anywhere, anyhow,
witness to the spillage of blood,
as Actaeon, whom she has loved,
or the idea of him, who has made her unchaste,
is disembowelled, whose brave head, as she sees it,
lies ludicrous on the sandy floor.
She would light up the forest with candles, if she could,
wear his head like a headdress of candles,
so that wax and blood was intermingled,
would drip to her shoulders in rosy tears.
And yet, with her cold stare, now,
Artemis at her shaking side,
patron of childbirth and chastity,
the double-voiced nature of her own creation,
with a miraculous stirring divorced from her body
scratches out words with a stick on the floor.
And the empty-eyed sky looks down, regardless,
as Faith dresses, rolls back her sleeves,
her eyes more knowing than she is telling
as she holds up a mirror to the goddess,
looks at herself, behind her, through it,
and on.

Quiet City

after Aaron Copland

So here I am in the dark wood,
not seeing life or love, for the trees,
wishing language could make of us something good,

the silence between us like the parted sea
as stern, in the blue light of the dash,
Will drives, refusing to look at me.

Then, out of the night, giving shape to our passage,
a line of music spills out on 3,
a trumpet of velvet rising from ash

as we slip with a gear change, a glance, through the quiet city,
unstrung, unlovely, but awake to movement's curve and bend
as I roll down windows, let air meet the body.

The city's left me spellbound,
opened me to a still magic: the ferrying river's riffling intent.
So we balance in the moment, lost from language, without God

or gods as music speaks at the silent heart of us. It's a sudden shift
as rift becomes raft, live, love.
I'm learning not to measure myself against it, the wish for the spirit

to burn open my mouth, to break me open or somehow move
me, for the night like a gift of myrrh, instead to spill
its ordinary perfume, as rain begins to fall on distant roofs.

Symposium: The Geneticist's Dinner

Tonight the talk's of twins and clones
a parlour game of metaphors to illustrate
the double helix of DNA.

Will has some things to say.
And because I've published a book,
a staccato treatise on cloning ethics

and our perception of death
– last year, a lifetime ago –
I'm expected to respond.

I try hard to remember a line of thought,
reel in the Virgin Mary,
Athena sprung from the head of Zeus,

the Groundhog Day of our human frailties,
anticipated but unfelt,
the fake promise of perpetual life,

but my sentences, like some decomposition,
lie like a corpse, are eaten away.
Before we leave, Nate Devine, confident,

a white-haired man with a tongue of glass
I remember from the funeral
asks if I'll give his faculty a talk next month.

Carefully, I look at him.
He's like some well-dressed dazzly god.
I take his card and say I'll call.

He bothers me with his eyes and laughs,
touches my arm like he's known me forever.
My cheeks redden for a moment

and then Will is there, and because I wanted it
we're walking home. The conversation's lifted us up
and for the first time in what seems a long time,

there's an alignment of the body and the mind.
Later we interrupt the night, the stars,
the kiss and the bend and heat of us.

And because everything, these days,
comes down to death, I remember
the canopy of stars, the four poster

both coffin and confessional where he told me
of the burial he'd have, hostage to nothing
but air and light – a slow dismemberment

on the roof of the world, the smell of cedarwood and pine,
cleaned flesh and bones hurled up to the vultures –
those holy birds I'd learned to love.

Beatitude

I sing in praise of single things –
of spirogyra, starfish, hydra and amoeba,
chlamydomonas, protozoa, of plankton, aphids,
dandelions and waterfleas,
their simple replication.
I sing in praise of sea squirts, strawberries,
the whisperings of the aspen tree;
sing, too, the earthworm, its hermaphrodite wriggle,
the complicated gender games of clownfish,
the honeyed urgency of the unfrail bee.
And praise too, the heroic rabbit,
her cheerful lesson of reproduction,
those charts we drew in blue and red
in third form biology. Praise also
sperm and ovum's heady clash,
the headstrong ram that tups the ewe.
Let me equally praise the love between men,
the love between women; praise the foetus' kicks
on a colander heaven,
the sperm blown fresh in the mouth
of the lover, humming with life, electricity.
Praise rub and touch, ungainly hump,
the cool pipette, its righteous offspring;
praise, too, responsibility. Praise our desires.
Praise our desires to know and not know.
Praise all our progeny, the empty womb, the full.
Praise the will to become, love's credo.

A Second Sighting

I'm walking from Paradise Street where I left the car
when something changes: a droopy cloud wanders
across an uninked sky. Mothers with their kids in
buggies, stroll. Hawkers hawk, shoppers shop.
A seagull catches me with its yellow eye.
Sunshine dizzies me with its sudden wink.
Then everything says Mara. *How do I know?*
Even like this, the long coat, the hat pulled low.
I take her arm, and as she turns
my heart does cartwheels down a thousand steps,
slalom on a wintry piste.

Then

She takes my arm, says "Ssssshhh,"
pushes a note in my gaping pocket.
Her dark eyes are cool as a church,
fixing on mine, both query and quest.

Who's written this strange yet familiar script?
Who's following who?
Then she's off, and I'm left with her whisper,
a mark on my arm where her grip was too tight,
handwritten lines on an unlined page.

Night Drive II

What I love at night is that sense of departure,
the recklessness of an enormous soul
and all the threads of life undone.
I might be going anywhere
as the radio speaks in tongues, untuned.
The Bluebird clears its throat,
and borrowing Will's mobile,
I leave a scanty message and my number
with Erica as I drive, digits punched
like stars in the galaxy,
my new address a welcome prison tag.
Those little helpers, sunshine pills,
I've left in a drawer in a former life.
Maybe silence is the voice of God,
the breeze that floods the empty bedroom,
the scrawl of the unmade bed.

A Visitation

Here, in the patch of darkness in the Bluebird where I sit,
Liverpool opens like a rent in time. The centuries elide

to a collage of water, newspaper print.
The songs of the slaves with their branded foreheads

rise to the heavens in a shift of pain,
and then the refugees take up their song,

abandoned in an unknown port.
Choleric children shake and cry.

The angel of history throws back her shoulders,
her violet eyes look forwards and back.

And for the first time in a long time I feel that I could weep
as daytime's colours slip

inside each other, disappear.
I press the buzzer as instructed,

and the slow world turns.
I give a last look back at the roughed-up night,

hold its memories close:
a street lamp, a dog bark,

orange, unearthly, bleak.

Limbo

For a while there's no movement, and no answer.
This rattling's the stenographer alive and remembering,
moving on silence and Canto V,
words bashed like braille into my head.
Then the door clicks a funny double click
and I'm in. Was it always this quiet,
with only the flickering heart
for company, walking fearfully into the dark
to meet the living dead?

Talking about the Weather

Was never on the cards, but she looks at me
with a look that blames the world.
"It's so cold in here," she says, shaking,
despite the weight of hair, her oddly androgynous
beautiful head.

Against Empiricism

I'm not sure exactly what I want,
searching for signs of life.
I feel like Saint Thomas slipping his hand
into the wounded side of God.

Chez Nous

She floods the world with light
and my eyes dilate to successive rooms
of highly-polished tables, chairs,
a room of Baby Grands....
She's sleeping in a storeroom;
stacked-up haphazardly on shelves
old pots, cracked jars; there's a
rising smell of creosote and polish,
the whiff of joiner's glue.
From a peeling plaster wall
a stag's head looms.
His glass eyes glint. Beneath him, half-asleep,
the hound. From beneath the lop-ears
a pair of doggy eyes look up.

Her words the only sound:
"The less I say the better," and her small, pale mouth is set.
In a strange domestic moment
she offers me a cup of tea, hands me scissors
and a tarnished mirror, bends her head
to light a cigarette. Her face is clouded
for a moment in the smoke. There's little enough
to show she's here: a rucksack with a change
of clothes, dog-food in tins, a toothbrush,
a notebook, a dulled Swiss Army knife.
At a table, in the corner,
are papers bundled, tied with string,
and a fountain pen, sharp as an arrow,
dribbles ink onto a blotter,
a wreath of flowers
etched in its glinting nib.

The match smears the silence, a falling star.

"You'll just have to trust me. I need your help."

The Haircut

Am I saving her life with stories, or is she saving mine?

I take the hair in a trembling hand, slice it to the nape,
then start to layer it, bring it closer to the scalp.

It smells of borage and camphor oil,
falls to the floor like a twist of apple peel,

spelling out words with a life of their own.

Second Look

She's taller and broader than I'd thought:
like Artemis the hunter god,

chaste and secure in her life without men.

The Answerphone

I'm fiddling with the mobile's keypad,
when out of nowhere Erica's voice rings clear:

"Call me," a sigh, and then
a voice

I almost recognise:
"News on Mara."

The voice of glass makes its arrangements.

We are all gone into a world of light.

Belief

There are things I want to believe.

In the absence of prayer I think about love.

Promises to Keep

Midnight, and things are slowly sinking in.
My head as light as an astronaut's
when behind me, out of the nowhere darkness,
there's the rev of an engine, a shout of lights,
and before I know it
a balaclava'd face looms large,
its hands at the wheel of a low black car.
I throw myself back on the warehouse wall
as night reduces to a stab of pain.
I feel the Bluebird spin as it carries a blow,
note how a fracture line of pink graffiti
spells INNOCENT on the sooted brick,
then look to a sky empty of planets
as slowly I reach in my pocket for the keys.
I'm going to shout up to Mara then change my mind.
I crunch two painkillers from the glove-locker's hoard,
take a swig of flat Coke. My hand trembles
as I start the ignition, shift through the gears
as we limp towards home. I'm alive, amazed,
nursing my pride, my car's broken wing.

Doubting Will

And how do we come home,
I ask myself, moving beneath the lintel
bringing the outside in,
dropping car keys on the mantelpiece
abandoning my jacket to a chair,
Will's phone returned to his empty pocket
where even now it shakes me with its stare.
Somewhere a tap drips, riddles away
its slight sad song. I pull a beer from the fridge
and the kitchen brightens as I lean against
the counter top, run my hands through my hair.
My lips are cool as a ghost's on glass.
How do we find each other again, I wonder,
carefully locking doors and windows, flicking a switch
so the stairway softens with a lamp's pale glow.
I watch my hand on my chest as it falls and rises,
as my lungs blossom, as I slowly exhale.

Faith

Will's fast asleep, buried in pillows,
cocooned in the pastels of our wedding quilt.
I watch how his body moves,
the moments of being that make him, still.
I think how his life is his body as I pull his body
closer to mine. What dream is this?
What science that pulls the body's airs and gases
unaware? What electricity
that brings us in a moment here?
The look on his face like a sleeping soldier
in Piero's *Risen Christ*.

White Nights

I'm a leper that sleep avoids:
my cropped head festering in the pillow,
pupils narrowed by the tilted anglepoise.
In all the detective novels I've ever read,
like Oedipus, the protagonist
just has to know.
Is every tragedy so closed?

Quizmaster: Starter for ten.
How many Chandler novels can you name?

Contestant: *The Little Sister, Lady in the Lake,
The Long Goodbye.*

Quizmaster: Poor show.

A Bout de Souffle

Breathless as the pill-dreams leave you
I'm left with what might be real or not:
Mara, shrunk to a tiny automaton,
balancing on my trembling eyelids,
slipping down my shoulders, leaping to the floor.
She shins up my knees like reticulate sorrow.
Her palms are bleeding.
There's an arrow in her heart.

Amour! Amour! she laughs.
Her face a stone that's fallen from the heavens.

Her wings thrash a hailstorm, blow the night away.

A Dream

Last night I saw the future's ghost,
Its face was dimpled, eager.
It smiled and sucked but could not rest,
I asked it to draw near.

As white as snow, as black as jet,
It hovered in the air,
Plucked at my lips, my hands, my heart,
Warming the stratosphere.

As red as blood, as fresh as bile,
Its tongue about my ear,
It whispered that it now was time
To undo pain and fear.

It shimmered, glittered, floating near,
I felt its pulsing heart,
Yet when I touched its open lips
It quickly disappeared.

My hand was marked with wonder,
A stain bled from a flower,
My fingers like bright stamens,
My palm the pollen bower.

Perhaps it was a vision
That slipped before my eyes
And moved between this world of mine,
And what is not categorised.

Or else it was a trembling thought
Escaping from the brain,
The mouth amazed to open
To a voice that's not my own.

I had not sought to harm it
With arrow, shot or knife,
Unlike the albatross it lived
And living it was life.

Some said it was some female god
Descending from above,
Making a genealogy of souls
From her idea of love.

Others a life in utero,
Gametes hurled into the several worlds
Where male and female slipped away
and couldn't be recalled.

Sprung from a head in brilliance
Like a – collision – in the sky,
It was a melody of differences,
A snowflake drifting by.

It looked behind, it looked beyond,
It brought an eerie calm
As if the world was in my hands
And soothed a raging storm.

And through the hawthorn blossom
As my tears disturbed the night
I saw it wander through the sky
Radiating light.

Its edges smeared with brilliant dust
It scorched its silent way,
A chemistry of splitting cells
A bright infinity....

Decisions

And then my waking up, a slow arrival
at a face, the brushed and suited blue
of morning, a damp kiss pushed

on my still-parted lips. *Sweetheart.* A quick departure's
caught through half-closed eyes:
a shoulder and a trouser leg,

a ghostly polished shoe....
My dreams are spilling still,
fall from my eyes like pennies, creatures

now, condemned to crawl in dust and corners,
dropping from my mouth.
The last squats on my chest and croaks, a

bright fire-bellied toad,
the heat and weight of which becomes enough
to burn the cool white sheets, take down the house,

erase the road, as flames run up
the street-lamps/blazing torches,
duplicates their orange glow

this sudden heat and untold fury,
bringing me round, with a gasp, at last,
settling in a line of sweat across my brow.

Following Will

I watch as he strolls across the university car park,
swipes his ID through the hesitant lock. Minutes later,

a small black Audi – behind the tinted glass
the driver like an arctic fox – silently draws up.

The porter, who knows me, nods me through.
I watch him through the glass partition as something

startles him, and he stoops to recover his fallen keys –
St Peter groping in the dark,

eternity, or the way into heaven, spilled from its fob like
                              sycamore seeds –

A Confrontation

Still-life, freeze-frame. An office, innocent as a pot-plant:
Nate's room. Blue letters on his door.

Will has his head in his hands, a stack of photographs
beside him. I watch through dirty glass.

Here's Mara caught on camera, pale and thin,
back-dropped by concrete buildings daubed in
                                        Chinese characters.

Is this Shanghai, Beijing? Beside her half-clothed children
are playing in the scrubby grass. My thoughts race on.

From this doorway in the empty building
the strip-light threatens in its blinking repose

and Rach II plays to our brief encounter.
Nate gives his ghostly, unchanging smile

as I enter the scene, wondering even as he says it
if this is some terrible double bluff

dividing first from last, the sheep from the goats:
the woman who died, the woman I found

not a ghost I'd refused to believe in, but met,
not Lazarus, or some fierce angel,

Not Mara, but her twin?

Clone

after PM

As *The Comedy of Errors* becomes *Twelfth Night*
and *A Stolen Life* becomes *The Double Life of Véronique*
and *Menaechmi* becomes *Amphitryon*
and *Invasion of the Body Snatchers* becomes *The Stepford Wives*
and Mike Yarwood becomes Rory Bremner
and Marilyn Monroe becomes Madonna Ciccone
and Megan becomes Morag
and Dolly Parton becomes Dolly the Sheep
so this becomes you

As a Partridge in a Pear Tree becomes the One True God
and Eight Maids a Milking become the Eight Beatitudes
and Eleven Benevolent Elephants become Lovely Lemon
                                        Liniment
and No Motor Response becomes Obeys Commands
and "Do Geese see God" becomes "Dogma: I am God"
and the *Collected Poems* of Li Po becomes the *Celestial*
                        Empire of Benevolent Knowledge
and Confucius becomes confusion
and Moy becomes moi
so this becomes you

As the Neolithic becomes the Paleolithic
and *Alice in Wonderland* becomes *Alice Through the Looking Glass*
and *David Copperfield* becomes David Copperfield
and *Opportunity Knocks* becomes *Stars in Their Eyes*
and The Byrds become A Flock of Seagulls
and Melanie Klein becomes Calvin Klein
and the angel in the house becomes the angel of history
and George Bush becomes George W. Bush
so this becomes you

As Mandelstam becomes Mandelson
and concomitant becomes commitment
and the King of Siam becomes Kojak
and the pea-flower becomes the black-bellied honey lover
and the madness of George III becomes Queen Victoria
and identical twins become mother and daughter
and affect becomes effect
and cwifer becomes quiver
so this becomes you

As Finisterre becomes Fitzroy
and Skin and Blister becomes Bricks and Mortar
and the good twin becomes the bad twin
and *Schmalz* becomes *Schadenfreude*
and Artemis becomes Diana
and *The Day of the Triffids* becomes *Gardeners' World*
and a shot in the dark becomes a shot in the arm
and vagina becomes penis, flowering in the shadowy womb
so this becomes you....

Liminal

I hover in between the spaces –
accident, coincidence, and truth –

Nate's expression benevolent, shrewd,
locked like a magnet into mine.

And Will upset, his features rearranging.
I imagine him the father of my child.

And all the time, like a pulse, a voice in my head
says something doesn't ring true. Why?

Because of something I read in Nate's cold eyes.
Mara, gone to the bad? Mara, like a phantom, gone.

III

Above Us Only Sky

Everything's still. An orchard of turf and stone, as I run.
Does thinking show me how to feel
or feeling help me how to think?
What is to be done?

I pass a gravedigger,
a woman in a headscarf with a face of tears,
standing by a common plot.
Is love the only game we play
with light and salt and air?
Is it only the pull of the earth
that learns to hold us down,
the spaces between grass and sky
we've always known are there?

The crime scene's yellow tape
reminds me. The white tape
of her absent body. What is this strange
return, a dangerous compulsion to repeat?
To slow-mo, rewind,
have the woman who's not Mara
hoisted by some unlawful force,
turn to the camera in surprise
as the arrow flies backwards,
launches out of her. What do I want?
For words and worlds
to unwrite themselves?
Years split beneath the soil,
glitter like dew-fall in the shivery grass,

paper and circumstance suddenly blank.

A Vacillation

Erica's on the sofa with her feet up when I finally arrive.
She gives me that look I'm getting used to,
directs me to the bathroom where I do the test.

There, twinned on a strip of white plastic
like a miracle I walk across,
a drunk on trial,
arms stretched out, without a wobble,

life,
a thin blue line.

Warehouse Fugue

We say we want to buy a piano
which I sit and play

haltingly at first, and then
forgetting myself,

the weight of my forearm pushed into the keys
so notes resound throughout the warehouse.

I play to the bar-line in my head, and then repeat,
Go back to sign.

Erica, however, *faux distrait*,
makes like she's looking for the loo.

"We'd a classy gent from the hospital in here."
She makes polite enquiries.

But even then I know.

Square One

I rest my head on the Bluebird's wheel,
as Erica, rooting in her copious bag,

hands me a softbound notebook and that fountain pen.
"Found this," she grins

with a look that says
I believe you, at last.

It's what, a diary?
Times, places, dates,

fragments of poems
Mara's copied out.

One in particular snags at my heart:

*Living had failed and death had failed,
and I was indeed alone.*

And there as I look,
the date I found the body –

Feb. 11th – eerily blank.
Underlined, the 17th, tomorrow.

In Chinatown the New Year celebrations:
the lion who does the

lettuce-eating dance, the
dragon dance that binds the people

bringing luck and happiness into the streets.
Already Will had filled the house

with plum blossom, narcissus,
a bowl of kumquats in the hall.

That's where I want to be,
trusting, alive, lost

in an odour of fruit and flowers,
and a sudden life inside me

I'd like the chance to tell.

Good Cop Pays a Visit

And I wonder why he does this,
sugaring his coffee generously,
handing me a sheaf of papers.
"Let's think of them as a large red herring."
It seems I'm off the hook for now.
He's asking lots of questions, still.
How long has your husband known Nate Devine?
And Mara, how well did she know Nate?
Were they friends or colleagues, would you say?
What would you say to the layman
was the nature of the work?
Dr. Dupin brought us a letter, has serious concerns.
"I've reason to believe your life,
your husband's, are in danger."
(Does he speak to a script?)
I'm losing the plot, haven't time or space
to think how I want my story to go.

A Call

The phone call comes, as I thought it might:
Nate, elegant, easy, always shameless.
And I play along.

The patter, the silences, carefully executed,
beautifully planned.

We agree to meet,
"It's a bore," Nate drawls, "but bring that husband of yours.
This time at least. He tells me you've something I'd like to see."
He laughs.
Mid-day in Chinatown,
The Ming Kee, a tiny restaurant we've eaten at before.
"Much more of an authentic experience, wouldn't you say?"
And then, "Wear that dress," he commands.
"Like hell," I think, but wait in the pause,
then slowly put the receiver down.

Year of the Horse

We're both bulked up in bullet-proof vests,
Good Cop and Bad Cop materialised
into something more than CID.
Outside a stall sells paper windmills,
pendants for double-happiness,
fortune cookies, rings of jade.
I lose myself for a moment to the crowd:
an art student whose dreadlocks reach his knees,
two Chinese girls in silk, tiger-dragon,
cherry blossom, ribbons knotted in their hair.
A grey-faced man marks bets, props himself
against a wall; two boys in shirts,
one blue, one red, scuffle with a ball.
Peace through the four seasons!
Strong body and health!
May your wishes come true!
The parades, the crowds, the noise, the dances
have begun. And then
like something walking out of myth,
pulled from a vase in the British Museum,
in an elegant movement from start to finish,
a familiar figure reaches for an arrow, loads a bow.
As Nate looks up, he's realised too late. *Mara!*
Seconds after there's a marksman's shot.
A splattering of firecrackers echo in the street.
Year of the Horse.
And blood is all we know.

Take Two

For the second time I'm left with a corpse:
Nate with his arms stretched out,
his face laid down. A woman's voice
shouts in Chinese. And, like a miracle,
the archer's disappeared.
A man in black wearing a baseball cap
swears, "Glanced her!"
pushes across the stunned and weeping tables,
follows her out back.

I look to Will, but he's gone too.

I sit there, speechless.

On my upturned hands, on my throat,
blood mapping all the untidy routes of life,
the veins and arteries
that lie beneath the skin
like trembling tattoos.

An Ending

How far can a dying woman run
amid the sounds of firecrackers and ambulances,
helicopters, sirens, the sudden brilliance of sky,
a small encroaching sun?
How far can Will, her best friend, follow,
and that dog, and those men, hot on their trail,
hounding a dying animal?
I'll let her go this far – past the Millennium arch
imported from Shanghai, failing now
as she skirts the Blackie, flying like the goddess
or the muse she is. Some poetic law of justice says
I'll leave her here: her breath coming fast but faint
on Hope Street, as I set her down
on the steps of a cathedral. *Let her die,*
there in the arms of a man who can't save her,
stemming the bleeding with his hands, his shirt.
Leave them be, framed by stone, looking up at the sky,
and a figure of Christ looking out at the city,
his arms embracing the theatres and restaurants,
the students and prostitutes, the crown-like peaks
of another cathedral, the seagulls, the river,
the skyline, what is beyond.
And this man with a woman in his arms.
Let's stop up our ears to those
last words between them.
Let time give them their moment,
whoever they are.

A Change in the Weather

Green shoots spike the frost
like secrets, promises that haunt us.
Bulbs push through the earth.
The umbrella silks of their brilliant colours
are their own grave: for all flowers
are flowers of the dead.

The Lantern Festival

We've filled the house with candles.
Time enough for roaming the streets,
tonight is our own. The threads of the story
are unravelling. And even now, Will says,
he isn't sure, which one of them was Mara.
Sisters who for thirty years hadn't
known each other, finding each other
a birth and death of the self, somehow.
But tonight the house is dancing to our light.
Grief sits, quelled for a while,
half-asleep, beside the snoozing hound.
Erica's here, with her day-old baby,
born in a pool as I crouched beside her
watching the face of her new son rise,
his tiny fingers dancing in water,
as he stares at us with some sweet surprise.
Blessings, little one as you softly feed. And little girl,
sucking your thumb beside your brother, curl up,
be at peace. Sleep for a while on these fire-side chairs.
Shadows flicker. And time begins.
Will throws another log across the fire.
A life flutters and turns inside me.
Elsewhere I've started to imagine.
Words spill across an empty page.

Relics

for Will

Different in shadows now, we look on at the evening,
the river like the name of someone unremembered,
a freckled arm, uncovered, a hemisphere of constellations
trailed across the sky. And so the soft straightforward night
begins with snowfall, snowdrifts – or do we just imagine that? –
as winter's ending colours us, imagines us as people
we have never been. And though a thousand different stories
quiver in a moment – a hand unclasped, a darting word unsaid –
I don't look back. Familiar in a dream
somewhere, my cheek pressed to your shoulder,
our lives grow up between us. Like the glistening bones
of martyrs, saints, you hold about your person,
I remind you, as we drive, "This is our tale,"
and words our only keepsakes of the Bluebird's journey home.

Afterthought

for my daughter

I am following with my finger the blue veins
that travel from wrist to stoop of palm
as you lie now, little milk-drunk carcass,
in an accident of sleep. This is what mothers do

or what I've learned to do, to search your body
for signs of life, wary of pulse and breath
as all the time you follow me,
your mouth, insistent, through the night.

See! I have pressed the soft vowels of your imagination
and made them part of me. They pull me open, stitch me up,
your animal grunts and hungry gestures –
so much a noise that might come from my own mouth,

I can't tell us apart. When I do, daughter, I'll admit, I'm lost,
my new body wandering the forest,
dropping trails of bright stones
till I find you again, a new friend in an old place.

And for how many nights will it be this way,
this slow process of making and undoing,
the soft osmosis of your fragile body? My willing you not
to slip away, turning my own blue veins

to ice? I watch sand gather at your eyes' corners,
shadows making your face from nothing,
those eyes, which might turn any colour,
flickering, half-open, in the pages of your sleep.

I let them rise inside me, birds cased in glass.
And all the while snow falls, depositing on lawns and roofs
its subtle metamorphic chemistry.
Days drift to your smiles.

And I watch the pink coil of your ear,
the snub nose of beginnings;
count to myself in this lonely country
the hoots of an owl, a line of trees,

the bright rings of your growth.

from *Burying the Wren* (2012)

Burying the Wren

I kissed you at the corner gate,
our breath warmed with whisky and ale

and thought of that small brown bird
the Wren Boys brought:

soft as the hairs behind your ears –
so cold – the wren on the pole in her little box –

the fluttering breast you longed to touch.

A Dream of Constellations

When the months that were left could be held in our hands
I wanted to speak, but I could not. The astrocytal cells
that formed and grew inside your brain
following heart lines, speech lines, bedding in,
bringing you visions, disrupting your speech,
brought us a night that was suddenly known,
but not as itself. And so, like a dream about to be spoken,
silence buried itself in me. In this new pitch,

the navigated darkness of our life,
this telling and untelling of the world,
Time sped and slowed. The constellations shifted,
bringing us messages in particles of dust and light.
Together we looked up to the sky
as Ursa Minor became the headless bear,
the twin sons of Castor and Pollux, unexcellent, unsweet,
buried themselves beneath the earth,

and Vela's sail unfurled, became ragged.
Sagittarius, the archer, staggered wounded,
ripped his arm on a jagged star, unnamed for this instant;
together we wept for Berenice
with her one breast, with her shorn-off hair.
And as Time was slinking, doing its business,
the fiery empyreal nature of things
became the thing on which we most depended.

It was a new world, our night sky,
and I'd like to think the story of what lived between us then
expanded in the moment of our looking:
charting new maps in the darkness, allowing us to trust
that we might live by the light of the stars and their
reseedings, those wild celestial fields, which
hovered in the dashes and the dots.

After You Died

The night would not give in to me –
or something inside me would not yield.
The great harness of love I was wearing
stiffened in my shoulders, was held like a bit
between my teeth.
              Last night
I woke and the moon was there,
her old romance of self-reliance and inconstancy.
And though my children in their turn
woke up to frantic dreams, were held,

brought back to bed,
she was there, her face full with a fierce singing.

And the dark again became a place
of sleep, a wild thing cohabiting.

Dogwoman

after Paula Rego

No one can love this horror, no one can want it.
I'm crouched between my own thighs,
with my dog heart and my dog soul. For now I'm a woman
brought up by dogs, bitch in the muck and the blood and the dirt.
For once, now, I've got no words, and look –
I'm trampling my bed, I'm baying at the moon.
And no one can hear me, with my skirts pulled up,
head back as my eyes roll. Look. I'm swallowing sorrow.
No one can hear me in spite of the howls.

★

I am lying on my back, my legs outsplayed.
That would be my dog-look, now, I'm giving you,
my half-cock, something askance and going to hell,
take me/leave me, inbreath, outbreath.
Trembling, I'm all upturned. Heart-hit, flesh-bound,
saying *love love* in a ring of devotion.
Here's my dogbelly with its small pink teats.
I'm waiting for the pressure
of your well-shaped hand.

★

Now dog's the divine. Strange thought. Dancing on hind legs,
head to one side, and the face of her master. Dog sudden, well-met.
Dog sitting, dog listening, dog running with big joy
and ghost dogs on the fields now with her. Dog blur,
hellhound, dog shaking, hare-bound; dog in the wind, sky-bound.
(Once, attendant in my blue dress, I hadn't the words to call you back.)
Dog in the snow, dog in the sea. Dog glorious, glories herself.
Dog racing with gleam and thunder. Best friend. Neither
fish nor fowl. Just for this moment hound bliss.

★

Now dog sleeps, dead to the world. Dog faithful. Dog tired.
Dog whose faint stink, dog-breath, dog with her lip curled, under the dog star
is dog waiting, dog at heel. There's no one to love
this sleeping dog. Dogsuckle, dogwash. Dog with her master.
Dog in a manger. Dog cradle. Dog holding.
Here now with her lover's body. Upstairs. Downstairs. Dog now
with her dogheart split. Rough courage. Dog mutter.
Dog pause. Moans, stirs.
Words now are never enough.

★

Dog tricks and the memory of dogs, dogs dreaming
and not in colour. Dog fetching, dog on a leash,
dog watching, dog weeps. Dog fond, dog mother.
Dog sniff. Dog holler. God of dogs, dog love.
Dog sent to bed in deep disgrace. Dog shock, piss, squalor.
And joy, dearest, tail wag. Dog rhythm, dog riff,
dog's domain and death's dominion.
The body's frame's not enough for itself,
these pale fires of horror.

★

Flea-bitten, dog-eared. At the centre there's a hole, or rather rent,
a tent-flap in the wind. Dog blood. Dog mess. Dog foaming
at the gates of hell. And, where words will neither cure nor reason
dog's here, fur-matted, nose wet. Lap dog, dog of the dead.
Wide-mawed. Tongue lolling. Dog in the dark destroying the world.
Dog killer, dog doper, dolling out medicine, taking her pills.
And who in the world could not love a dog? Dog rhyme. Dog bold.
Guantánamo dog in her orange jumpsuit.
Girl on the mountainside, dog girl at her bones.

★

Now I've a look of something else, leg drawn to my shoulder.
Dog woman whose dog limbs quiver; dogwoman
and my teeth are bared. A plastic collar might do the trick,
to stop me gnawing at flesh and fur. Dog alert and
no one to touch her. Dog gesture, rat-catcher.
Dog least likely. Dog outstretched. Dog-snout,
snarling, hollering. The flowering armpit of a gramophone.
So here we are, in the veiny dark. Here's
the moment of pain when the music holds.

★

Had I once known my dog self – whelp, cur – the
dog skull, dog rose, hair of the dog from shoulder to paw,
good dog/bad dog from which I came, wouldn't I now
in this stiff chair ask you again, letting things slip,
my head resting on your furry pelt, head lifted
to the pink of your maw? And how would I know,
and would you be glad, of this dog bright
pricking her ears? Dog in the mud. Dog in the dust.
Wouldn't I ask you not to go?

★

Dog gentle in the good night. Dog lost, hunkers here.
Dogwoman, dogsoul. Breath escaping
the bone cage, faster. Dog refusing to leave her master,
dog gentle, dog love, dog left in the wild machine
of dog grizzle, dog slobber, holding you now
it is over and over. Licking and weeping,
a body cools. Woman loving. Dog gone. I am
speaking/not speaking an unspeakable prayer.
And now I am kneeling, dog alone.

★

Alert in the darkness, head to one side, dog's very still.
And then I see her at her own side, waiting.
Particle, matter. Dog in the moonlight.
The trees cast their shadows. The day hunkers down.
From the black leaves of night she creeps, very slowly. Quietly,
with her dog eyes closed. Out of blood, out of debris,
snuffling, singing, settling skirts and shaping
the emptiness, dog howling, dog waking.
Doggedly dogging, dog being born.

★

This slow love as snow falls becomes elsewhere
the fierce heat at the core of ourselves. Dogs jumping up,
tangled in wildflowers. Dogs in a waterfall, dogs at the beach.
Dogs reading books under African starlight. Dog with her nose now
pressed to the window. Dog in the cold. Dog in the dark.
Dogs crying and frisking the limitless reaches.
Dogs on their cliff edge, not looking down. And
Love in the things that can't be unbroken. Love in the skies
where I cannot yet follow. Love, in these strange times, passage of souls.

Trilobite

Remember, as a child, how someone would shout *Catch!*
and too old to refuse, and too young not to –
the body's coordinates not quite set

this object, moving in an arc towards you
somehow created you, trembling, outstretched?
That's how it came to me, this trilobite,

a present from the underworld, a stern familiar
hopelessly far-fetched. What it wanted from me
I never knew, its hard parts being its only parts,

the three sections of its crossways nature
cephalos, thorax, pygidium
as later, now, I've learned to call them,

carrying a memory of itself like water
as my fingers moved on its captive body,
the feathery stone of its cool guitar.

It reminded me of a woodlouse, too,
the honesty of small, friendly things.
But the metallic gleam of its smoothed edges

were taut and innocent as an unfired gun.
So it bedded in, leaving behind a gleaming trail
as a biro bleeding in a pocket might,

a puff of ink from a hounded squid.
And my skin shimmered
with its silvery threads, and my breath quickened

as it wrote my body, left a garden of knowing in damp tattoos.
The further I threw it, the closer it came.
Sometimes, alone, I'd ask it questions

stroke it like a secret pet
How deep is the ocean? What's the blueness of blue?
How is the earth as you lie inside it?

It would reply in a voice both
high-pitched and enduring, or
whisper like a ghost till only silence remained.

And left me only when I'd learned to love it,

small as a bullethole,
in the place where it pressed itself,
its fossil colours close to my heart.

Last night, unable to sleep,
it nudged its way back into my life,
pulling me from the fragrant pillow

to perch once again on my naked shoulders,
to drop like a coin in my offered hand.
Beside me, my husband slept.

And the fact of its presence, its subtle truth,
was something to touch,
like the wounds of Christ.

Its transformation as I went to kiss it,
a wafer on the pushed-out tongue.

Truffles

The Umbrian black truffle,
a delicacy in these mulish towns,

was born, or so the Romans had it,
when lightning struck the earth,

secreting a nugget of heavenly fire
in oak or hazel woods

whose altitude and climate,
calcerous soils, combine to breed

the truffle's strength,
its heady auras known

by sweating housewives, perfumed chefs
to make electric any humdrum dish:

a fungus potent, so we read,
as the pheromones

of two wild boars – known also
for their sense of smell –

whose butchered testicles emit
a scent more dangerous to some

than Japanese beetles, gypsy moths
or Circe with her plaited hair

who tosses acorns, feckless men,
into the hot Aeaean mud.

More pungent, then, than mountain goats
whose cheese we daub on rounds of bread,

the amoretti which we dip in wine, or,
hemmed with rosemary and mint,

the sunflower fields where,
like the truffle hunters, too, this burning

afternoon, we root out treasure for ourselves
until we've harvested each spore

from armpit, neck, from groin,
enthralled by subterranean gods

who now make dogs of us, or swine,
till we lie senseless in the dirt,

hearts splitting in the heat.

A Chinese Lacquer Egg

Something is beginning. We feel it in the raw edges
of our dreams, our bodies hostage to light, to weather.
It is filling us with the weight of summer
which floats like helium through our wintered bones.
We wonder at it all, surprised by warmth, a sudden downpour –
the ruffled line of birdsong, a forgotten bulb
forcing its way through sodden earth towards the sun.
Or this Chinese lacquer egg, which appeared one morning
in my outstretched palm. Beyond the sound
of aeroplane or train, as we drift asleep, hands cupped
to the pillow, it shares its oval mysteries. Listen!
Between breath and silence it is showing itself.
In these shortened nights it is not unlike rapture,
an unworded prayer its indelible hum.

Shaved Fennel with Blood Oranges, Pomegranate, Peccorino

im Thom Gunn

It's one of those moments, the radio on,
light creeping through the kitchen
on an early summer's evening
and then the sudden piercing, a voice announcing
that you're dead. It mingles, now,
with the smell of fennel,
blood oranges, and ewe's milk cheese,
green seeds and lemons, pomegranates,
a dish served up, that night, a funeral plate for one.
It is food to take the winter out of all of us,
calling us as even now,
with its muscular flexing in foetal turns
I call my own child on.

Couvade

Like that tribe of South Americans
who raise a sympathetic magic
from a woman's growing foetus
piercing themselves in unspeakable places
and hanging under torture in the rafters,
bird's eye witnesses in agony
at the moment of their baby's birth

you've taken this pregnancy to heart
as daily you grow listless, unsteady
in the mornings, muttering
in your afternoon sleep,
craving fruits or nursery foods,
bland textures, carbohydrates

a sweet tooth running amok
limbs thickening, waist rounding out,
your auburn hair like the mane of a horse –
but as Strabo observed, looking better
than most, with darkening areolae
high-flushed cheeks, the smile of Valentinus.

Daughter II

Blake's angel, what makes you?
blood, bone, mineral? the black space
that creates the universe, would

if it could, suck everything in?
Sometimes
I hardly dare look, the night

losing its face in the senses
as you, with those owlish eyes,
little ribs, not long since

shocked into light
and an appetite
and your damp hair like feathers

nuzzle in beside me,
no one to answer,
or to answer to. Only

an unlearned joy when you wake
which is ours, your breath on my skin
enough to stop a heart,

to darn the threadbare morning.

Aderyn yr Eira

(Starling)

Against the green-black of the sleek night sky
the burning love of a mother and a daughter:
stars made into snow, and vice versa.

Slugs

Each night the slugs have found a way of getting in.
They slip through cracks, inhabiting corners,
edging up table-legs, walls, or chairs.
With their slug etiquette, slug gestures,
are they silently dreaming of lettuces, hostas?
Do they elegise greenhouses, commune with their dead?
Or fantasize brethren on distant planets?
What mistakes do they make, and how will they tell us?
Do we ask their forgiveness? Do they imagine us saved?
Of their psychobiographies will I ever be sure?

Occipital horns conduct in the darkness.
They know nothing of envy, nothing of blame.
In the gastropod inchings of their midnight seances,
the slow rehearsals of molluscular dance,
they're themselves absolutely, beyond imitation.
And their silvery cast offs Isadora's
just at the moment in the silvery moonlight
when she sheds her scarves to a million stars.

Hallucigenia

(i)

The room where I imagine you, my eyes unclosed
to its supposéd windows, floors, eventually misleads me
so that even now we're years ago with different lives
and dumb voyeurs to this: two bodies
catching at each other, light.
Such faithlessness for us becomes a kind of death.
What helps is this: that pleasure's
something made from love as well.
Denying it, taking it up, would hurl us out of time
away from our more equal loves
and everything outside that can't be fitted
into just one life/two lives.
And so a look that stirs can make belief itself more right,
more real, in fact, more dear, and no impediment.

(ii)

Ok. But as we're in that room I've brought you to,
our stanza out of time, out of our depth, let's say
on the muddy floor of the Burgess Shale
where velvet worms and arthropods
whose spiky backs and stumpy legs,
whose compound eyes imprint
themselves, *hallucigenia*, in rock,
let words, which like the fossils
make a house for us in lexical delight,
open the world to reimagine us,
to catch the imprint of our softened parts
which as my mouth now, line by line,
is emptied into yours, becomes a different silence
from the first, in commas, dashes and full stops.

My Grandfather's Tattoo

On sunny days, his shirtsleeves rolled,
he'd cover with a sticking plaster –
like the wound of Welsh he wouldn't give his children –
the blue-green inks of anchorage, the shame.

Daughter III

It's peacock, she says, and holds up the stained-glass page to the light;
or, pomegranate, she decides, returning to colour
the jewels of its hundred eyes.

L

Some mysteries are never solved: the tongue of flame,
the rolled-back stone, the body's weight
when it walks on water; or even the tale
of the Capuchin priest who for fifty years
wore the wounds of Christ, was drenched in the odour
of holy blood, his body healed at his last confession:
Maria! he whispered, bowing his head,
dying the death of a little bird
as he stood before the gates of heaven.

Which takes me back to that night in San Andreas
and the barbell I found, caught like a thorn
between mattress and sheet. Or was it a dream –
the blue of her skin between ligament and bone,
her arm bent like the letter L, as she washed your feet
with her hennaed hair? The blemish on your palm
between headline and heartline, a faultline,
like her name, or the scent she wore,
the line of a song you won't remember.

from the *Songs of Elisabeth So*

I notice, now, that you've lost weight,
your hair is cropped, your body somehow smaller;
and square and unfamiliar, the lines of your dark suit

that show your gait has found a new lopsidedness,
the way our year-old son in shoes
adjusts his body to – and us the heart –

new freight
and finds me, as I wait here, only sad.

And I don't want, I find, those flowers
that used to spring up with your look,
then fade and darken at your passing.

The corridors are singing with your hurt.
Take songs away, take flowers away, take too
the gentle artfulness of your restraint.

★

You call me Elisabeth, which I like,
Elisabeth *So*, Elisabeth *Please.*
And you undress me in a dream.
And so you tease....

Forgive me these,
as your words, my love,
unhook, undo.
And do not move

until I'm there spelled out with you.
The bed is awake with us at last.
Your name is one
I will not speak.
Don't ask, don't ask me to.

★

Whose mouth is this in the roomy darkness,
whose hand is this that flies with mine,
who sails with me in the room in the darkness,
whose body slips with mine through time?

Whose voice is this that calls me, calls me,
who runs beside me like the wind,
who holds me as the ocean pulls me,
who holds me, word to word, a rhyme?

Tell me, what shall we do with this hour of abundance?
What shall we do with this hour of wonder?
What is the best way to sing our praise?

I ask and ask but you will not answer.

My mouth is yours – if only you'd answer,
to prove the darkness and the silence wrong.

★

We're out of season, out of luck,
the day pot-boiled to its unlovingness.
So go.

Like a wronged god, or a ghost.
I never wanted you.
For we are not a rhyming pair,

we are not in the one breath,
not the morning's sudden clear air.
We are not the surge

and swell, the ocean's rhythm.
We are
not even a plywood plane thrown up into the sky;

ours is not this kind of gladness.
We're so unlovely and so small.
Know that as we lie together here.

★

It was the only blessing that I asked you for,
of leaving me unnoticed –
like the earth might tree seeds or a rouged leaf
in its fall.

Instead, you give me nothing,
catch me inside your coat
to see if you can catch my breath

steal me, my soul,

which slipping through me, in an instant, rises up
and hovers near the smell of you.
.
The thumping of your chest to which I'm otherwise immune
has left me on the wind's breath, now.
It was the blessing that I asked you for.

Instead you leave me trembling here, a feather.

*

The gentle artfulness of your restraint is what, of course, I love;
the gentleness that as I sit beside you
I can't prove –

just like the look you give which, though I see,
I must refuse to catch and hold, as I imagine you'd
hold me.

But my hands, beside yours in the sunlight, can't refrain
from singing as I hold them in my lap;
and then a thousand birds begin to rise.

They sing and fly in the singing light
and the room is suddenly full of their music.
And I do not care that they will not listen.

And I do not care that they will not stop.

Shrub & Willow

Shrub's heart was a box, a certainty.
While Willow played, let out her hair to the rheumy breeze
Shrub was inviolable, a taut high wire.

Willow on the banks of the still river, raised her head
to check the sadness.
How like that mermaid with human feet
was her walking through silence, her dancing on glass.

Shrub was a sentry on the steps of the house.
Shrub was anger, Shrub was despair.
Perhaps Willow was love, an hysterical air.

Yet blood ran between them. And how will it be, my unlikely pair,
O my Willow, my Shrub,
in the forest's night when I find you there?

The Fetch

When she came, her eyes shielded against the light,
it was as if we'd always known she would:
her dark hair and her eyes like apple pips.
From whose head had she sprung?

She was calling me in the silence of puddles,
cloudfall, a rise of starlings to the darkening nights,
sap sticky in the dew.
Twice she came and then a third,
her heart exposed, espaliered against her ribs,

her face pressed to the window.
.
I watched her that last time as she walked across the room.

She carried in the pockets of her velvet coat
bittercress, dogviolets,
and, like the memory of a shape of a book,
a solitary duck egg, blown,
its melancholy blue.

The Box

I'd asked for calico to line the box
and though you'd passed

so far from self, and I
still wandered, something was at rest.

On the funeral day, I came again:
your lips were cold, your eyelid stitched.

And later it was Pam, not I

who laid the turf from Mayo at your feet,
the lilacs on your chest.

A Scattering

I am standing by the waters where we've let you rest:
ashes, candles, seven roses set like seven boats

into the lough. The rain has stopped
and our daughter dances.

Where is our son?
Way up high on his great-uncle's shoulders.

A swan's wing, limp, instead of my arm.
I'm a bride to silence, these smaller spaces,

the mist like breath on the landscape's glass.

Chinese Lanterns

Bright crêpe on summer nights,
a carnival, of melancholy heat,
a row of pumpkin-headed smiles.

Their skeletons are metaphors
to wear against the dark –
who wear their loss barefoot

like sad fluorescent dancers.

Peony

Such intimacy when I press into the darkness of its heart:
as if it were a friend of mine
– like love — like death –
I speak to it of this and that, I furnish it with whispers.

Moon River

They're not the words I'm thinking of,
but the tune comes back the same.
And all the lives we've never wanted.
Your face in the huckleberry river.
Holly Golightly running through the New York rain.

Kinks

Hitting a hairpin bend in fourth, I'd be forgiven
for calling you everything under the sun, our rock and roll
on the empty road, as life, now, flashes before me,
moving me from fear to love.

And would I be forgiven, too, in the darkening room,
for seeing last night a likeness in you
to that honey-bear the Kinkajou?

Who, sipping nectar from a balsa-blossom bud
had your face, and so took my breath,
dusted with light as it was, and pollen.

Ellipsis

And there I found myself, more truly and more strange.
                                        —Wallace Stevens

I had started to think of the skin ego,
of *Women, Fire and Dangerous Things,*
the lost books, fluttering, opening their wings like veins....

                    ★

Perhaps it was a false start, the veined blue
remembering of a breast, the scent of milk
in that photograph, the coil of your double crown as you fed.

                    ★

But words like bandages were slowly unravelling...
and somewhere I was becoming the dreamwork of my life,
every room in the house now blunted

to an irrational fear of knives, maybe,
the glittering wage of the umbilicus,
the navel of the dream.

                    ★

And the blue heartstopping pulse at the wrist
was insistent as a rhyme
unstitching itself...

the red stain of the past
on my improbably stretched-out hands.

Stillborn

These days, I lie awake,
picking from beneath my skin –
a reassembling in the dark –
two gleaming eyes, a beating heart,
pink on the cheeks like a daisy's edge, my brother:
fragments of tooth and bone.

Letter from Marrakesh

for Kate

The swifts are flying across the medina...
a sudden storm has blown pink sand across the souk
and Alex wonders do you want an ostrich egg?

A wild dog ate, alas! the lonely tortoise in the garden.
An old umbrella doubles as a parasol.
Our children's texts like bird prints in the snow....

In the Djemaa El Fna you wander through the crowds:
the fire-eaters and storytellers, tooth pullers, acrobats....
These days are all that is ahead of us.

Come soon, you write, come soon....

Each night, a great white owl
like the moon, missing its step in the sky,
swoops down to drink the silver swimming pool.

Meteor

And this is how everything vanishes,
how everything that vanishes begins,
the hinged moment looking forwards and back.
Like that night when we sat with the back door open,
the summer distilled to the scent of jasmine,
the scrape of cutlery, the chink of glass.
A robin stirred in the dusty hedgerow.
Clothes held our bodies as a mouth might a kiss.
Then the meteor brought us to our feet:
a stripped atom, trapping electrons
to excite the darkness with its violet light.
I remember how it disturbed the heavens,
burned against the air to leave no trace.

Persephone

Some days it is simple,
the way outside turns inner –

the fall towards light,
the pull of the weather.

This is love's work –
the way I've learnt again to slip inside my dreams:

to hold my face up to the rain,
move from one world to another.

Tom-Tom

A last gift from my father.

And I think of him now as I slip through gears:
the satellites are calling, the coordinates are set.

Where we are going and how we are getting there
is all we need to know... and this is what he most remembered:

my propensity for getting lost.
Is it his voice trailing from the heavens?

Like one of Ovid's beasts transformed,
the tom-tom like a brave's heart beat.

Burying the Wren

(Coda)

So these are the dog days,
when the sea boils, and the wine turns sour;

when the sky thunders, and the house cries out:
Dearest, you promised you'd be near.

One day, you'd just fetched up.
Love me, I said. Who else was there

to step into my thorny heart,
who knew enough in your half-life

of soul-mess, blather, to take my hand
in the dark wood

and walk with me away?
Now this might be my hardest weather.

You call to me and call again.
O skittish I am all astray.

★

If I look up now when the sky burns black
perhaps I can remember this:

your way of leaving us and our long night –
love-blessing, liturgy,

the prayer of the unholy,
and getting you –

death rattle, heart-stop –
to where the struggle ends –

sending you in the longboat of your body
where worlds and words collide, was not

the end of love. Yet love
you've been with me enough,

so I must let you be, remove myself from the
cool earth, where weeds will blossom, rivers run,

your pyre of turf that burns
along a drift of speedwell and bogthistle,

primrose, pimpernel and vetch,
where rain will learn to fall once more

and lightning bring its electricity
to animate the uncaged heart.

Here, where a wren sings, flirty in the alder,
in the long hot days of May,

when you are three years gone.

from *And You, Helen* (2014)

*Between the terrific noise of the guns I can hear
two hedge sparrows making love.*
                                        –Edward Thomas

Prologue

Can the loosestrife make us a home?
Can the skylark, stuttering, sing
and be known to us? Can the bee, creaturely,
dodging the breeze? Can the dragonfly
with her wings of glass? Can the bitter leaf
and sweet grasses, grass seeds,
meadowsweet and chickweed. Can the ants
and woodlice, windblown burrs?
Can the spider, assembling herself,
pull threads of silver one to another?
Can celandine, catkins, an orchard
bound in mistletoe? Can the moth,
alert at our edges? Can a butterfly
rising and gliding in the powdery nettlebeds,
can the shadow of the oak tree
casting itself from green to black?
Even as the sky darkens can the hare,
stilled at the field's edge, nervy, watching,
bring us an answer? I answer yes.
And love hunkers down,
shows us her great mercy.

1.

At first, she sees nothing.

Darkness rubs at her – star-blasted, dream-filled – knocking her
                                                    sideways
from love,

out of sleep. None of this knows itself. Slow. Forming. Now it is
morning and so there's a shift, when dark is an opening. A heartbeat
on darkness. Pulse. *Pulse.*

This is her mind: connecting with feeling

with thought   with a memory   memory of thought.

Loosestrife. Nettles. She fumbles in spaces, can sense
                                        in the half-light
the breath of her children.

Her body takes root. Her body takes hold.

Roses blacken in a jug at the bedside. Ash in the grate
                                        remembers its fire.

Now it is morning. Yet still there is nothing.

Nothing

but a space beside her.
            Nothing,
            but a space inside.

2.

The oak tree knows the field, the bend of its shadow to the grass.
It knows the sun's path -- passage of blackcap, starling, rook --
how to clutch a song and nest it in leaf. It knows the ant that
labours up grass blades; a stag beetle glinting, passage of worms.
The tree surrenders its shadow to shadows. Oak tree and field converse
in the shadowgrass. Here is how shadows bend, here
is where birds rise.
                              Birds   rise   up.

(Had the night known its own self --- darkness ---
it would have opened wide its mouth, afraid.)

Two men walk across the field. Her heart's beat like a missed step.
August wears ghost selves. And the shadow of one
                              keeps on walking into shadow.
While the shadow of one
                    lies down.
                                                Pause.
Moth flutter
                    like shadow broken loose
                              carving grey in the moonlight.

First you hear rain, then you imagine it, seeing how the rain might
            drum at its brokenness.
                    Drums inside.

A man feels the dark field singing through his bones.

She feels it, too. Rain singing. Love singing. Here, now,
are its broken lines. Here, in a heartbeat,

the white explosion.

A body lies, thickening with mud. And the dead who are long gone
open up their mouths.

The rain. The field. Every small thing it owns.

3.

Where he is, stumbles.

Although she can imagine him, pulls lovingly a thread -------
his voice -------
----
silence

breaks in the listening,
widens, stretches.

A hare quivers like an unearthed wire.

Hush.

While the field moves she's complete in her listening.
Rain on the roof makes eaves a dull listening.

Then thunder dulls, and the sky splits.
She's dreaming of journeys and trains through the darkness.
Elder, dogwood, flaming maple.

----------- pulls at a thread.

4.

As this old tin bowl holds water for washing, it holds, too,
                                    the memory of water
As her body holds the memory of -----------,
                                    she holds, too.
As a gun holds the memory of its firing,
as the earth soaks up water, sends it skyward;

as the skylark ---- as the fieldfare, sparrow, blackcap, rook ----
as her body holds his body,

as their slow, deep movements ----
he holds too.

As milk burns in the breast, remembering the tug of ---
as their bodies are a bridge, and children call to her
out of their sleep ----------

as her collar bone, as her pelvic bone, as her ---
everything

holds

as the horses ---------
as the ------
as the --------

as she wakes from a dream
as shrapnel, as mud.

5.

Where she is, stumbles. Her fingers move to the edges of her body,
negotiate the space at her clavicle. She holds the full weight
                                                    of her breast in
                                        hands.
She cannot feel much more than this.
When she wakes, she reaches for the space. Is it always like this?

Each step, each step ---------
as if each bare foot on the wooden stairs
might suddenly explode.
                        So field edge touches sky edge.
So a pair of sparrows squabble in the corn stooks.

Somewhere, between the greying field and the dusk dark,
between grass song, her whisperings, and tree song,

the talking of the leaves,

a body hangs.

Here is the moment between living and dying,
the space beyond and the space inside.

She stretches out her limbs and -----------

There is a conversation taking place.
The space beyond the space inside.

6.

Does the breeze pull a thread of hair across a brow?
Does the movement of the blood around the body

      stoppered by the earth's stop
                        run to a halt?
Do the lungs expand, after death, to this?

And is silence then its own sound?

Does she wait now for an exhalation?

Does a breath come at the very end, overdue?
Does a wren caught beneath a hedgerow suddenly appear?

Fieldfare, sparrow, rook.

There's blood at the throat. *Whose throat?*
His body is perfect. Only his heart,
as if caught in the split of a second.

He gives her a look. *Pause.*
The skies light up. Is this the way she might imagine him?

Poems feather in his pocket.
Birdsong. Here, is the stillness of --------

Robin or redstart, called palely to his palm.

7.

The memory of a memory. That last night returns to her. Fragments
melting in nudges of firelight.

His hand touches, without somehow touching,
                                        any human part of her.
                                        It is like this.
                                        ----- this slow gorgeous
                              climbing and gathering,
                                        this entering, this being in

White clover, yellow bedstraw, milkwort.
She drops a glass. And now her face, as if something at her heart
had spilled. Or the crack, singing like an ice floe in darkness,
            widens   holds.

What she holds,
        she holds for their children. But now there is breakage.
The terrible shifting ocean of herself, let out.

8.

Loosestrife, nettles. She'd unbuttoned her blouse,
letting her clothes fall loose to the waist,
then pool in a circle --- shoulderstaps, underclothes ---

She makes his body, as she guides his hands, a poem.
The sun a covering, the sky a covering. Their two bodies

in one movement
                    a poem in the grass.

9.

She remembers the day he turned tight on his heel,
took a gun in his hand to walk out to the woods.
The children's eyes blackened,
wounds in the darkness
                          and her own heart split.

She wonders at the fury of endurance.

Where to place love?

Sinew   curve
edge   vein

Love
      cooks, digs, sews, binds, smoothes, irons, cleans.
                    wrenching from tiredness, dirt,
                                  a tenderness.

When they lie together in the night, it is something like this --------

Pulse.

Rain furies,
      dances, sings.

If he sees the world through her eyes, then she sees the world through his.

10.

He has gathered her up in his old great coat.
Can he carry her, she wonders, like the girl she was,
in his officer's coat, with his freshly razored hair.

Mosses grow on the furzy green; her red dress tears
like a wound, in a wound.
He has gathered her up and will sing to her

under the shadow of the deep-breasted oak.
Listen! This is the sound of his tread on the stairs.
He has gathered her up.

My arm in yours, my hand in your pocket.
You must walk, he laughs, with her hand in his pocket,
as if in your dreams.
And the dead who are long gone

open up their mouths.

Let us open up our lips. Let us show forth our -----
Star-blasted, dream-filled.

White clover, yellow bedstraw, milkwort.
She opens her mouth to a dark field.
She opens her mouth
                    to a thousand leaves.

11.

The oak tree knows the field.
She walks now, in its shadow. Nettles, meadowgrass.
All, now, that has travelled between them:
sweat, semen, blood, milk, tears.

Leaf shadow touches grass shadow.
A child mutters in the breakages of sleep.
First you hear rain, and then you imagine it.
She dances with him. Leaf shadow touches grass shadow.

And you, Helen?
She begins --

                    When I walk I walk with
                    the white shock of an
                    explosion.

                    When I love

                    When I walk I walk with
                    their clean white bones.

                    (*We hear the song of the thrush*)

I.M.

Sometimes at Easter we'd drive west,
stopping, makeshift, at our curious stations:
once to put a bet on a horse –
once, slowed behind a whole village, a man
dragging a man-sized cross. Now Easter
is come round again and I stand once more
by a restless lough. Your body's ashes drift:
Carra, Corrib, the shores of Carrowmore.
A landscape has become a conversation;
mountains, godlike, touch my godlessness,
Croagh Patrick stained by pilgrims' feet.
Darling, what did I leave when we left you
where sky and water meet?

*

An old love is a kind of promise.
In the first rush of new unholy orders
there's a wish to make a body limitless.
Now here's a longing for my breast
to meet a mouth, for you again to slip your hands
inside my heart and with a turn of limbs
to bring a rhyme of colour to my cheek.
Owl hoot, fox call. A phone rings
in a distant house. How to be one
in this strange equation? We drive together
in the dark. I mark a simple prosody
in making tea. Later, in each other's ghostly arms,
the radio will sing us both asleep.

★

The bed is drenched with the sweat.
Beyond the sunshine and the open windows
I name the birds who draw an endless song.
I see us now reflected in that mirror.
You lift me up, we hold each other down.
Is it too much, you ask, not letting go.
You stack up logs beside the fire, bind up
our cottage beams in mistletoe.
And how could my body not cry out –
harmonics of our loveliness?
Your voice sits in my mobile phone.
It was our perfect happiness
to make your self my own.

★

I drifted into trees. The arborist's banter
when I ask him how he came to this.
He names ash, alder, silver birch, trees
that would suit this back yard better, tells me to listen
to the family of wrens who've nested
in the neighbours' eaves. What would I give to become
this Daphne, rooted and evergreen, desire doubling
each year in upward growth, beneath the seagulls'
melancholy bleat. In the next door yard
a flock of greenfinches, like leaves, take flight.
Their gorgeous synchronous song's a torment.
The common laurel which I plan to fell
today can stand for love, this hell.

★

Into this breakage and this breach
its roughened magic, love approximate,
an urge comes to fix and mend, to search
to cure myself of sickness, to detonate
myself to life, to cure myself of love:
stitching for one who cannot sew,
mendings for that which we can't mend.
I gather a coat of burrs and nettles.
You look up from a book
I never watched you read.
Love, what was the gift
you thought you were giving?
What in the end do I have to leave?

★

I raise from *YouTube* the songs of birds:
skylark, nightingale, play them, teacherly,
to a sleepy class. On my desk are letters,
birds nests from the garden. Blackbird, linnet.
songthrush, robin. Would you know, I ask,
what Keats knew, Clare, matching a bird
to a pattern of knowing, taking a stanza
from form to flight? To be twenty
and begin again! To love madly,
and for so long! Hairs rise like
golden feathers up my arm. Love,
in the dreamy reaches of our brains,
your absence asks if love was ever wrong?

*

'House of the Singing Winds'.
At the foot of the Sugarloaf
blackthorn spikes and brides
the hedgerows, crows gather
in the upward fields. Now grief
is written in their dark alignments,
sorrow in a nearby field of horses.
In an absent moment I can still
look up to see you there, call out in sleep,
or pull two glasses from the press.
Daily, text messages erase.
I turn my back on you until you leave.
I'm relearning the metrics of being alone.

*

I cannot show you the English gardens,
now you are gone, not the magnolia tree,
breaking extravagantly open, not cyclamen,
narcissus or delphinium, the fiery tulips
with their mouths' soft spillage,
a liturgy of spring that steers to summer –
foxglove, rose, peony, geranium –
as I sit here with our son. The stepping stones
steal through the grass, the tilting water clock
that measured out my childhood's gone.
I put myself to my own test.
It is a prayer demanding answer,
asks what I would be warden of.

★

Perfection in execution, a repetition like desire.
Here is the joy of shifts and modulations.
Bach's cello suites demanding our attention.
Like anything, I say, you have to practise love.
Now I have missed the sight of us together,
watching a thousand fieldfares smear the February air.
Were I to practise love again, I'd hold the memory
of the morning, hand in hand, as we watched
a fledgling robin open up its throat beside the river.
Bach's cello suites shout out for my attention
as March now runs to April. I hear a robin's song,
remembering how, down empty lanes, a thousand fieldfares
(so it seemed) rose up, to splinter winter's air.

Acknowledgements

'I.M.' first appeared in *The Poetry Review*. My thanks to first readers and editors over thirty years who have encouraged and supported work, especially at *Poetry Wales*, the *New Welsh Review*, *The Poetry Review*, *London Magazine* and *Poetry London*. Thanks also to Arts Council England, the Arts and Humanities Research Council, the Society of Authors, the Ledbury Poetry Festival and the University of Liverpool whose generosity at crucial points allowed periods of writing time and invaluable research leave. Deep thanks to my family in Liverpool and Ireland, and to dear friends and collaborators. Amore more ore re.